NINE ESSAYS

ARTHUR PLATT

NINE ESSAYS

by

ARTHUR PLATT

With a Preface by

A. E. HOUSMAN

CAMBRIDGE

AT THE UNIVERSITY PRESS

1927

CAMBRIDGE
UNIVERSITY PRESS

University Printing House, Cambridge CB2 8BS, United Kingdom

Cambridge University Press is part of the University of Cambridge.

It furthers the University's mission by disseminating knowledge in the pursuit of
education, learning and research at the highest international levels of excellence.

www.cambridge.org
Information on this title: www.cambridge.org/9781316601693

© Cambridge University Press 1927

This publication is in copyright. Subject to statutory exception
and to the provisions of relevant collective licensing agreements,
no reproduction of any part may take place without the written
permission of Cambridge University Press.

First published 1927
First paperback edition 2015

A catalogue record for this publication is available from the British Library

ISBN 978-1-316-60169-3 Paperback

Cambridge University Press has no responsibility for the persistence or accuracy
of URLs for external or third-party internet websites referred to in this publication,
and does not guarantee that any content on such websites is, or will remain,
accurate or appropriate.

THE author of the papers collected in this volume was one whose published writings, though they show the rare quality of his mind, do not portray the range of his studies and the variety of his accomplishments. Nor do these papers themselves complete the picture; but they have been recovered and put together that the world may know a little more of an uncommonly gifted man who was not much before its eye, and whose reputation was highest within the narrower circle which knew him well enough to admire him rightly.

It is not certain that he would have consented to their publication, for he must have felt that they bear some traces of the circumstances which called them forth. University College London, like many other colleges, is the abode of a Minotaur. This monster does not devour youths and maidens: it consists of them, and it preys for choice on the Professors within its reach. It is called a Literary Society, and in hopes of deserving the name it exacts a periodical tribute from those whom it supposes to be literate. Studious men who might be settling *Hoti*'s business and properly basing *Oun* are expected to provide amusing discourses on subjects of which they have no official knowledge and upon which they may not be entitled even to open their mouths. Platt, whose temper made him accessible, whose pen ran easily, and whose mind was richly stored, paid more of this blackmail than most of his colleagues, and grudged it less; but the fact is not to be concealed that these unconstrained and even exuberant essays were written to order. The only one which he allowed to be printed, and that only in a college magazine, is *Aristophanes*. Two however have a different origin and were composed with more deliberation. *Science and Arts among the Ancients* is an address delivered before the Faculties of Arts and Science in University College on a ceremonial occasion, the opening of the Session in October 1899; and the Prelection is one of those read in public by the candidates for the Cambridge Chair of Greek when it fell vacant in 1921.

John Arthur, eldest of the fourteen children of Thomas Francis Platt, was born in London on the 11th of July 1860 and died at Bournemouth on the 16th of March 1925. He was sent to school at Harrow, whence he went up to Cambridge in 1879, winning a scholarship at Trinity College. In the first part of the Classical Tripos of 1882 he was placed in the second division of the first class, a position which may have disappointed himself but did not surprise those friends who, whenever they went into his rooms, had found him deep in books which had no bearing on the examination. In the second part a year later he obtained a first class in Literature and Criticism and also in Ancient Philosophy. In 1884, like his father and grandfather before him, he was elected a Fellow of Trinity. This Fellowship he lost under the old statutes by his marriage in 1885 with Mildred Barham, daughter of Sir Edward Bond, K.C.B., sometime Librarian of the British Museum, and granddaughter of R. H. Barham, the author of the *Ingoldsby Legends*. Their children were one son and one daughter. For the next eight years he taught at the coaching establishment of

Wren and Gurney in Bayswater; in 1894 he was chosen to
succeed his friend William Wyse as Professor of Greek in
University College London, and soon after took up his
residence about a mile away on the edge of Regent's Park.
He held his Professorship more than 30 years. In 1921,
when Henry Jackson died, he was persuaded to become
a candidate for the Chair of Greek at Cambridge, to which
few or none of the competitors had a juster claim; but he
was relieved when he was not elected, and it is certain that
Cambridge would have been less to his taste than London
as a place to live in. He would have vacated his office at
University College by reason of age in July 1925, but in
1924 he was attacked by illness, and did not live to complete his term.

At the time of his appointment some feared that they
were yoking a racehorse to the plough and that his duties
might be irksome to him because they could hardly be
interesting. Much of the teaching which he was required
to give was elementary, and he seldom had pupils who
possessed a native aptitude for classical studies or intended
to pursue them far. But he proved assiduous, patient, and
effective: only an oaf could help learning from him and
liking him; and with his best students he formed enduring
ties, and would inveigle them into reading Dante or
Cervantes with him at his house of an evening after they
had taken their degrees. Outside his own class-room he
was a centre and fount of the general life of the College,
most of all in the Musical Society and among his colleagues
in the smoking-room after luncheon. Nearer to his house
he made another circle of friends. He was a Fellow of the
Zoological Society, frequented its Gardens, and inspired

a romantic passion in their resident population. There was a leopard which at Platt's approach would almost ooze through the bars of its cage to establish contact with the beloved object; the gnu, if it saw him on the opposite side of its broad enclosure, would walk all the way across to have its forelock pulled; and a credible witness reports the following scene.

I remember going to the giraffe-house and seeing a crowd of children watching a man who had removed his hat while the giraffe, its neck stretched to the fullest capacity, was rubbing its head backwards and forwards upon the bald crown. When the object of this somewhat embarrassing affection turned his head, Platt's features were revealed.

In youth he had poetical ambitions, and his first book was a volume of verse; a smaller one on a personal theme was printed privately, and so was a collection, made after his death, of sonnets, very personal indeed, with which he had entertained and striven to ameliorate his colleagues. He early produced recensions of the *Odyssey* and the *Iliad*, in which it was his aim to restore, so far as might be, the original language of the poet or poets, and thus to pursue further that special line of Homeric study which began with Bentley and his digamma, engaged the acute but undisciplined minds of Payne Knight and Brandreth, and has left as memorials of its progress the editions of Bekker and of Nauck. Nothing could be more different, or could better display his versatility, than his other chief work, the translation of Aristotle's *De generatione animalium* with its multifarious notes on matters zoological. A slighter performance was a free rendering of the *Agamemnon* of Aeschylus into the prose of King James's Bible.

Among the Greek scholars of his country Platt belonged to that company of explorers whose leading figures, after the universal genius of Bentley, are Dawes, Porson, and Elmsley. Minute and refined observation for the ascertainment of grammatical and metrical usage was his chosen province; and his early investigations of Homeric practice were his most characteristic work, and probably surpass in value his later and more various contributions to interpretation and textual criticism. Metrical science, upon the death of Elmsley, had deserted its native isle and taken flight to the Continent: Platt was one of the very few Englishmen who in the last hundred years have advanced the study, and among those few he was the foremost. In conjectural emendation, like Dawes and Elmsley, he was shrewd and dexterous enough, but not, like Bentley and Porson, eminent. In literary comment he did not expatiate, although, or rather because, he was the most lettered scholar of his time. He stuck to business, as a scholar should, and preferred, as a man of letters will, the dry to the watery. He knew better than to conceive himself that rarest of all the great works of God, a literary critic; but such remarks on literature as he did let fall were very different stuff from the usual flummery of the cobbler who is ambitious to go beyond his last.

If his contemporaries rated him, both comparatively and absolutely, below his true position in the world of learning, the loss was chiefly theirs, but the blame was partly his. He had much of the boy in his composition, and something even of the schoolboy. His conversation in mixed company was apt to be flighty, and his writing, though it was not so, carried jauntiness of manner to some little excess. Those who judge weight by heaviness were perplexed and deceived by a colloquial gaiety, much less unseemly indeed than the frolic sallies of Dawes, but striking more sharply on the sense because not draped like them in the Latin toga; and it was disturbing to meet with a scholar who carried his levity, where others carry their gravity, on the surface, and was austere, where he might without offence or detection have been frivolous, in conducting the operations of his mind.

That he wrote little was the direct and natural consequence of his extraordinary capacity and the variety of his interests and attainments. He would rather improve himself than instruct others. He wrote on subjects where he could make definite and original contributions to the advancement of learning: otherwise he preferred to read. Greek was his trade, but the home in which he dwelt was great literature, whether its language were Greek, Latin, English, French, Italian, Spanish, German, or Persian. The best authors were his study, but his reading ran far beyond them; his curiosity invaded holes and corners, and his taste ranged from the *Divine Comedy* to *Jorrocks's Jaunts*. He followed his inclinations and read for his own delight, with a keen and natural relish, not a dutiful and obedient admiration of the things which are admired by the wise and good. Nor were his studies warped and narrowed by ambition. A scholar who means to build himself a monument must spend much of his life in acquiring knowledge which for its own sake is not worth having and in reading books which do not in themselves deserve to be read; *at illa iacent multa et praeclara relicta.*

Music was a rival of literature in his affections, and his

knowledge of the art and its history was almost an expert's. He followed with interest and understanding the progress of discovery in the natural sciences, and his acquaintance with zoology in particular was such as few laymen can boast. In conclusion it is proper to mention his vices. He was addicted to tobacco and indifferent to wine, and he would squander long summer days on watching the game of cricket.

His happy and useful life is over, and now begins the steady encroachment of oblivion, as those who remember him are in their turn summoned away. This record will not preserve, perhaps none could preserve, more than an indistinct and lifeless image of the friend who is lost to us: good, kind, bright, unselfish, and as honest as the day; versatile without shallowness, accomplished without ostentation, a treasury of hidden knowledge which only accident brought to light, but which accident brought to light perpetually, and which astonished us so often that astonishment lost its nature and we should have wondered more if wonders had failed. Yet what most eludes description is not the excellence of his gifts but the singularity of his essential being, his utter unlikeness to any other creature in the world.

A. E. HOUSMAN

CONTENTS

Frontispiece

ARTHUR PLATT

BIBLIOGRAPHY

Separate Works

Marpessa, a masque, with eight odes, by Arthur Platt. Cambridge, Deighton, Bell & Co., 1888.

The Odyssey of Homer, edited by Arthur Platt. Cambridge, at the University Press, 1892.

The Iliad of Homer, edited by Arthur Platt. Cambridge, at the University Press, 1894.

Aristotle, De generatione animalium, translated by Arthur Platt. Oxford, at the Clarendon Press, 1910.

The Agamemnon of Aeschylus, freely translated by Arthur Platt. London, Grant Richards Ltd., 1911.

Articles, Notes, and Reviews

[*C.Q.* = *Classical Quarterly*. *C.R.* = *Classical Review*.
J.P. = *Journal of Philology*.]

Aeschylea. *J.P.* xxxii, 270, xxxv, 86 and 332.
Aesch. Agamemnon. *J.P.* xxxii, 48.
The plot of the Agamemnon. *C.R.* iv, 98.
Agamemnonea. *C.R.* xi, 94.
The last scene of the Seven against Thebes. *C.R.* xxvi, 141.
Aesch. frag. 291. *C.R.* iii, 417.
ωραν etc. in Aeschylus. *J.P.* xxxi, 234.
Aetna 597 sq. *C.R.* xxxv, 29.
Apollonius Rhodius. *J.P.* xxxiii, 1, xxxiv, 129, xxxv, 72.
Aristophanica. *J.P.* xxxiv, 289.
Conjectures on the Clouds of Aristophanes. *C.R.* xiii, 428.
Notes on Aristotle. *J.P.* xxxii, 274.
Arist. Atheniensium respublica. *C.R.* v, 105 and 185.
Arist. De anim. incessu. *J.P.* xxxii, 87.

Arist. De part. anim. I, i, 14–8. *C.Q.* IX, 8.
Arist. Poetics, xxii, 9. *C.Q.* IX, 7.
Arist. Politics, I. *J.P.* xxv, 26.
Notes on Bacchylides. *C.R.* XII, 58, 138, 211.
Bucolica. *J.P.* XXXIV, 142.
Callimachus, Oxy. pap. 1011. *C.Q.* IV, 112 and 205, V, 41;
    Berliner Philologische Wochenschrift, 1910, 476.
Catullus, 11, Horace, Od. II, 6. *J.P.* XXI, 46.
Cercidas frag. 2, ii, 12. *C.Q.* VI, 43.
Empedocles. *J.P.* XXIV, 246.
Euripides, Andromache. *C.R.* X, 382.
Eur. Rhes. 720. *C.Q.* XIII, 153.
Herodotus, II, 22. *C.R.* IV, 48.
Homerica. *J.P.* XIX, 19, XXIII, 211, XXXII, 19; *C.Q.* XIV,
    123.
Note on Homeric scansion. *J.P.* XVIII, 120.
Spondees in the fourth foot in Homer. *J.P.* XVIII, 150.
On the fourth thesis of the Homeric hexameter. *C.R.* XI,
    152.
The augment in Homer. *J.P.* XIX, 211.
Duals in Homer. *J.P.* XXIII, 205.
Notes on the Homeric genitive. *C.R.* II, 12, 99, 149.
On some Homeric genitives. *C.R.* XI, 255.
Some Homeric aorist participles. *J.P.* XXXV, 128.
A Homeric idiom defended. *J.P.* XXVI, 81.
Homer's similes. *J.P.* XXIV, 28.
On Homeric technique. *C.R.* XXXV, 141.
Brandreth's work on Homer. *C.R.* VII, 107.
Notes on Reichel's Homerische Waffen. *C.R.* X, 376.
Iphigenia. *J.P.* XXII, 43.
ἀρειή. *C.R.* I, 280.
ἑκατόμβη. *J.P.* XXII, 46.
μέλλω (Homeric and Platonic uses). *J.P.* XXI, 89.
Notes on the text of the Iliad. *J.P.* XVIII, 126.
Notes on the text of the Odyssey. *J.P.* XVIII, 154.
Notes on the Odyssey. *J.P.* XX, 7; *C.R.* XIII, 382.
Bentley's notes on the Odyssey. *J.P.* XXII, 26 and 198.
The slaying of the suitors. *J.P.* XXIV, 89.

Theognidea. *C.R.* xxvi, 73.
Thucydidea. *J.P.* xxxiii, 270.
Thucydides, ii, 48. *C.R.* xxxiii, 63.
Virgil, Aen. vi, 567 and iii, 702. *C.R.* v, 837.
On a Virgilian idiom. *J.P.* xxiv, 46.
Xenophon, Oeconomicus. *C.R.* x, 382.
Emendations of Xenophon's Hellenica. *C.R.* xxxv, 100.
On Oxy. pap. vol. ii. *C.R.* xiii, 489, xiv, 18.
ἐγώ. *C.R.* x, 381.
On τε etc. with vocatives. *C.R.* xxiii, 105.
On the iambic trimeter. *J.P.* xviii, 161, xix, 146.
On the Indian dog. *C.Q.* iii, 241.
The Lyrceian water. *C.Q.* x, 83.
Split totems. *C.R.* v, 339.
Rendering into Greek elegiacs. *C.R.* xi, 70.

Reviews in *C.R.*:

Van Leeuwen and Da Costa's Iliad. ii, 174.
Edwards' Iliad, xxiii. v, 476.
Van Leeuwen and Da Costa's Odyssey. vii, 81.
Butler's Trapanese origin of the Odyssey. vii, 254.
Lang's Homer and the Epic. vii, 318.
Van Leeuwen's Enchiridium. vii, 859.
Butler on the Odyssey. ix, 56.
Way's translation of the Odyssey. xx, 60.
Herkenrath's Der Enoplios. xxi, 155.
Walker's Ἀντὶ μιᾶς. xxv, 16.
Meillet's Origines indo-européennes des mètres grecs.
    xxxviii, 20.

SCIENCE AND ARTS AMONG THE ANCIENTS

*(Opening of Session of the Faculties of Arts
and Science in University College,
London, October 1899)*

Science and Arts among the Ancients

IN addressing the Faculties of arts and sciences a person who is not even supposed to know anything but Greek cannot, as it seems to me, do much better than by giving a sketch of the relative position of arts and sciences among the Greeks, as regards their education. To discuss that question at all completely would be a matter of much time and would require an immense amount of explanation. A mere definition of the words arts and sciences as understood by the Greeks would occupy all the time available to-day. Still one may contemplate the lines of a mountain from a distance, and draw the simple outline on a sheet of paper with some profit, though knowing that on a nearer view those lines would assume different forms, be broken up into ravines and projections, and sometimes even run into one another without the sharp boundaries which appear from afar off. All sorts of qualifications and innumerable links of transition must be simply omitted by me.

Some years ago the representatives of science, waking up after a long period during which they had been ignored in education altogether, made very startling demands. They said that science was the one thing needful, that arts had had an unconscionably long innings and it was time they declared[1], that everybody ought in childhood to learn exactly what happens when a wax candle is burnt, because it was more useful than learning the accentuation of the genitive plural of παῖς. The representatives of arts and what

[1] Terms borrowed from the game of cricket.

is called a liberal education were equally fierce on their side—they said they had no notion of declaring before they were all given out, and in particular Matthew Arnold said that the chemistry of a candle and the accentuation of παίδων were both facts of equal value for education, but he would like to know what science could put in the place of literature. The noise of that controversy has, I think, pretty well died away—both parties have cooled down— Science in particular has largely withdrawn her claims to anything like an exclusive education—and the teaching thereof in public schools remains a farce—both sides recognise that they have no business to dictate to everybody, that what is one man's meat is another man's poison, and on the whole you *must* let people follow their own bent. In fact the question is really between two types of mind, into which the human race naturally divides itself—the artistic and imaginative and poetic which wants to enjoy, the scientific and analytic which wants to know. It is easy to call both bad names, but it is better not. In this College at any rate they dwell in perfect peace, and their language is unimpeachable.

The conflict, as I have said, is really one between two types of mind—only secondarily between different subjects. If we all had the same type of mind, the conflict of subjects would vanish. The history therefore of the conflict in ancient times is concerned *apparently*, but only *apparently*, with different matter from that with which it has been concerned in recent times. It assumes at first the form of a battle between poetry and philosophy. Later on philosophy splits into two main parts, science and what we now call philosophy in a more restricted sense, or mental and moral science and logic. This latter branch, what we now call philosophy, has got ranged on the side of arts somehow —and indeed philosophy proper is a somewhat ambiguous kind of creature, a species of *Volvox*, and stands somewhat between the two, the prey of both. As for mathematics, though they may now be included in an arts course, they are obviously purely scientific in reality, but as Aristotle has invented logic as an alternative for them we may look upon them from a distance with great respect and say no more about them.

Faculties can exist only in Universities, Colleges or some bodies of that kind which undertake to educate people, not Correspondence Colleges nor Imperial Institutes. The Greeks can hardly be said to have possessed anything which could be called a College, though the philosophical schools of Plato and Aristotle and others approximate thereto. And our third Faculty of Medicine was never brought into any connexion with the other subjects by them.

The Faculty of Medicine, indeed, has *always*, so to say, dwelt on the other side of the street[1]. In primitive times no doubt there was no such thing—I have sometimes speculated whether that is why Methuselah lived so long. Herodotus informs us that in Babylon if anyone was ill he was taken out and laid on the ground or propped against the wall in front of his house, and everyone who passed that way stopped to ask what ailed him and recommended him anything that he thought useful. How long any sick man ever survived this course is a question which Herodotus

[1] University College and its Hospital are on opposite sides of Gower Street.

does not raise. Nor does he state that anyone ever went back into his house.

In Homer also we are told that a physician is better than any other man at cutting out arrows and applying healing herbs. He is only *better*, but there is as yet no separate Faculty. But in Greece, at any rate in very early times, physicians wrote great text-books and killed men according to rule, and already by the time of Plato and even earlier the philosophers had marked off this profession as the only one with which they would not meddle. It is possible they did not know when a doctor might not be called in to them. The encyclopaedic Aristotle left them to themselves, and I believe that even Mr Herbert Spencer has done the same. Leaving this then aside, the first germs of the division of knowledge and education into two Faculties of arts and science appear at the time of the great awakening of thought in the fifth century before Christ, 2400 years before this lecture. The antithesis began between two classes of men who typified the two great aspects of the human mind, the creative or imaginative or artistic on the one hand, the inquiring or understanding or scientific on the other. The poets were the voice of the former, the philosophers of the latter. Philosophy in those days did not mean what it does now: to put it briefly it included all literature or written matter which was not art or history, and an enormous quantity of talk; but it also included rhetoric, which is generally counted to be an art. The name applied to the first philosophers was "sophist," a word of no bad signification at first—it meant simply a man who was notable for wisdom or learning, a man who, like Browning's Grammarian, decided not to live but know, not to enjoy but to think and analyse. Professor Ker told you a story in his Oration last Foundation Day about a certain unprincipled person who being asked what the sophists were like referred the inquirer to the Professors of University College. I have always thought myself that this was rather hard on the sophists, who were after all a body of very remarkable men. However that may be, at first the philosophers devoted their energies simply to speculating about natural sciences. They had no method for the most part—they simply sate down and made guesses, some good, some bad, a pleasant but ineffectual method of advancing human knowledge, still popular I understand among candidates. Then they began to turn their attention to the life of men; they taught rhetoric, they taught virtue, they examined and criticised the current ideas of mankind, and among other things they came across poetry.

Up till that time the poets had had everything their own way, they were monarchs of all they surveyed and their right there was none to dispute. The inspired verses of Homer were regarded as a Bible, appealed to as a final and sovereign settlement of every question. By a verse from Homer Solon is said to have disposed of an awkward political difficulty, just as the President of the Transvaal even now confounds Mr Chamberlain by a quotation from Isaiah or the Psalms—in Dutch.

In education also the poets were supreme. In those blessed days, a true age of gold, a young man was expected to learn nothing but what young women used to learn in England until recently. I have heard distinguished scholars wish that they had lived in those days. Music and poetry along with reading, writing and arithmetic—a *very* little arithmetic—these formed the whole intellectual education of the men who fought at Marathon and Salamis, who built the Parthenon and wrote the *Agamemnon*. Music and poetry always went hand in hand, and it is now quite impossible for us to understand the value the Greeks set upon music. To them it was not a mere amusement but the most powerful agent, or one of the most powerful, for forming character. It was of an excessively simple character, as we should now think; harmony in our sense of the word was unknown, counterpoint could still less be expected, and the instruments used were principally occupied with supporting the voice. Yet the effect wrought upon them by it was far beyond anything which we can now comprehend. Nothing perhaps can better make us realise the importance of music on moral training among them than a very remarkable passage of Polybius. Perhaps you will excuse my reading it to you in an English translation.

"Music," he says, "and I mean by that *true* music, which it is advantageous to everyone to practise, is obligatory with the Arcadians. Everyone is familiarly acquainted with the fact that the Arcadians are the only people among whom boys are by the law trained from infancy to sing hymns (and paeans), in which they celebrate the heroes and gods. They next learn the airs of Philoxenus and Timotheus, and dance with great spirit to the pipes at their festivals. Similarly it is their custom, at all festal gatherings, not to have strangers to make the music but to produce it themselves, calling on each other in turn for a song.... Their object in introducing these customs was not the gratification of luxury and extravagance. They saw that Arcadia was a nation of workers, that the life of the people was laborious and hard, and that in consequence of the coldness and gloom which were the prevailing features of a great part of the country the general character of the people was austere. And it was with a view to softening and tempering this natural ruggedness and rusticity that they not only introduced the things I have mentioned, but also the custom of holding assemblies and offering sacrifices in both of which women took part equally with men, and having mixed dances of girls and boys, and in fact did everything they could to humanise their souls by the civilising and softening influence of such culture.

"But the people of Cynaetha entirely neglected these things, though they needed them far more than anybody else, because their climate and country is by far the most unfavourable in all Arcadia. They on the contrary gave their whole minds to *mutual animosities and contentions*. They in consequence became finally so brutalised, that no Greek city has ever witnessed a longer series of the most atrocious crimes.

"I have had three objects," concludes the historian, "in saying thus much on this subject. First that the character of the Arcadians should not suffer from the crimes of one city. Secondly that other nations should not neglect music. Lastly I speak for the sake of the Cynaethans themselves, in order that, if God gives them better fortune, they may humanise themselves by turning their attention to education and especially to music."

So far Polybius.

When I consider the coldness and gloom of the metropolis, and the melancholy results which followed upon the Cynaethans' neglect of music, I feel inclined to hope that the practice of pianoforte playing may not entirely be dropped by *both* sexes in favour of the "mutual animosities and contentions" of the fierce struggle for a University degree. Heaven only knows how dreadful the results may be. Perhaps there may be one or two among my hearers who will be warned in time.

The decline and fall of music is indeed one of the most

remarkable phenomena in the history of education. It is a symptom of a great change, not entirely for the better. The reason why music was valued by the Greeks was its moral influence. *We* have made education purely intellectual and leave moral influence to come in how and where it can manage it. Briefly, all education began by being *moral*—and it has ended by becoming all intellectual. Hence when music is recognised at all by Universities and similar institutions (unless it is a mere accomplishment) it is studied as a branch of mathematics and nothing else. One is expected to know about thorough bass and the chord of the thirteenth and so on—as a part of general education it holds no place, and the practice of it is contemptuously relegated to the realms of deportment and dancing.

Aristotle himself, while considering music a most important branch of education in youth, actually forbade the practice of it in later life—he declares that "no well-bred gentleman ever sings or plays unless it be over his wine or for a jest." But the consideration of the ethics of music in advanced life must be left to my amiable colleague Professor Roberts[1]. It is time to go back to the fifth century before Christ.

Homer was backed up in a more philosophical style by a number of poets who wrote doubtful ethics in verse, chief among whom were Simonides and Pindar. These bards were quite happy to hitch the ordinary ethical ideas of the period into verses, to make with an air of profound thought generalisations not unworthy of Mr Tupper, and to contradict themselves and one another with the careless felicity

[1] Who had a fine voice, and was always called upon for a song after a College dinner.

of didactic poets or occasionally with the acrimonious politenesses of modern philosophers. But nobody at first cared to ask exactly how their various maxims were expected to square with the rude possibilities of actual life or even the airy fabric of a complete system. If one of them said "Money, money makes the man," and another said virtue alone can make one happy and keep him so— if a third extolled knowledge or genius—the public were quite content to quote them all indifferently as all of them equally infallible—they were poets—servants and prophets of the sacred muse—they *must* know all about it like Mr Kipling. To criticise them was as if one were to criticise the papers on general science set in the Matriculation Examination.

Great was the outcry, as may be well supposed, when the daring and impious sophist laid his hand upon the ark. Heraclitus of Ephesus, a man of unquestionable sagacity and depth of mind, and one of the proudest and haughtiest of men, declared that Homer ought to be flogged out of Greece. Such blasphemy must have struck the rest of the world with something of the same horror as Voltaire's *Écrasez l'Infâme* struck Catholics of France in the last century. Plato followed up the attack by another of a very elaborate kind. His assault was made from two distinct points of view, the one ethical and the other metaphysical. The stories told by Homer about the gods are immoral and disgusting, he said; therefore they cannot be true, because the gods are good. But if we should grant for the sake of argument that they were true, they ought even then to be buried in silence, the minds of the young especially should not be contaminated by such doctrines and by such examples, just as the University of London cannot allow Lamb's *Specimens of the Dramatic Poets* to be set for a B.A. In a well-regulated state therefore the poems of Homer will not be admitted at all; we shall confess his greatness as a poet, and it will be with the deepest regret—but—we shall inexorably exclude him from our gates. Moreover all poetry and all art of every kind is, when looked upon from a metaphysician's point of view, essentially a thing of a low and inferior kind. This world is a fleeting show, it is full of error and deception, a sea of perpetual change whose billows are never constant—if we desire *truth* we must rise entirely above it into a region of philosophic abstraction and pure thought, where there is no change, no storms, but truth abides unchanging—and one would think just a little dull. The phenomena of *this* world are but a bad imitation of the world of truth. But what does the artist do? He comes and imitates the things we see about us—the people we know in this life—his art is an imitation of an imitation and thereby is at once degraded. (I say nothing of the value of this argument.) How strange then it is to find the poets giving themselves such airs! How strange to find them talking as the lawgivers of mankind, posing as men who are somehow of a superior rank to ordinary mortals!

Plato himself speaks of the quarrel as one of long standing. If the philosophers proved by ethic, metaphysic and logic that the poets were no great matter after all, the poets retorted in their own way. They have always been noted for vanity and irritability, they are *not* noted for logic, and their method of defence is apt to degenerate into abuse and sarcasm and reiteration of their superior claims. They made sarcastic observations on the "rabble of over-clever heads," they wrote comedies on the philosophers and their ideal states and raised inextinguishable laughter at their expense—nay, they go on doing it still. Tennyson entreats other people not to vex the poet's mind with their shallow wit and assures them they will never be able to fathom *him*, and after over 2000 years Mr Swinburne takes up the cudgels for Aristophanes against Plato and defends the poet in language which really cannot be here repeated.

Education however has always remained in the hands not of poets but of—pedants and.... It was not Aristophanes but Plato who drew up the first scheme for a University course, and, as may be well supposed, the arts did not make much of a figure in it. Poetry was confined to the service of the gods—Sternhold and Hopkins were to replace Homer.

Music too was to have her wings clipped—all further progress was forbidden. Only certain kinds of music were to be allowed and those only the simpler and more archaic. One may illustrate his proposed legislation in this matter by supposing ourselves to be now forbidden to play any music except in the keys of A minor and C major, or to perform any work composed since 1759—I sometimes wish we were.

Philosophy in Plato's scheme was the final subject to which everything else was subordinate, and (as was natural considering his contempt for this world) he really makes education the preparation for another and a better life. Sciences, so far as he condescends to recognise them at all, are nothing but a preparation for philosophy and are destined to withdraw our thoughts from the transitory to the eternal. This being so it naturally followed that he took serious objection to the sciences as studied in his own

day. To take only one example out of many—the astronomers, says he, ought not to seek to know the exact course
of the planets—he would have been very contemptuous
of all investigation into their weight and their chemical
constituents—what should an immortal spirit care about
helium? No, the genuine astronomer will regard the
motions of the stars as only useful for leading the mind to
the contemplation of "those true revolutions, which real
velocity and real slowness, existing in true number and
in all true forms, accomplish relatively to each other, carrying with them all they contain: which are verily appre-
hensible by reason and thought but not by sight." It
sounds very pretty, very pretty indeed, and one is further
comforted to hear directly afterwards that such a plan is
"many times more laborious than the present mode of
studying astronomy."

From this instance it may be plainly seen that if Plato
had had his way the sciences would never have advanced
far. In effect Plato, like Bacon, wanted to lay down laws
for people who knew their own business better than he did.
His lofty superiority is better justified than Bacon's, no
doubt, because *he* did not pretend to be advancing science,
but his attitude quite reminds one of Bacon jeering at the
discoveries of Copernicus and Gilbert. His claims for
philosophy are in reality as outrageous as any that had
been previously put forward for poetry, or as those put
forward in recent times for science. All three have in their
turn said: "I am the only thing worth considering; sell all
thou hast and follow me."

And indeed if this world *is* so miserable a delusion as
Plato would have us to believe, he would be justified in

his claims. He was a sort of forerunner of the Catholic Church in the Middle Ages, which, like him, thought education ought to be a preparation for another world, which despised science, made art subservient to itself, and tried to stop all advances. Yet Plato was at the same time a curious mixture of the two opposite types of mind—in him the desire for knowledge of the truth of the universe was commingled with all the romantic feeling of the dreamer of dreams. He dwelt among cloud-capt towers and gorgeous palaces, and fancied that he was leading the human mind along the dry and steep path of knowledge. Over the cradle of the sciences he wove enchanted rainbows, mists of the morning which the sun was to dispel when it arose displaying things in the naked light. Despite his contempt for scientific methods he had an astounding insight into scientific questions. His dialogue named *Cratylus* was the first treatise on philology, and the acuteness of much of it is amazing. In the *Critias* he displays a capacity for solving geological problems, and a breadth of view, which justify us in calling him probably the greatest geologist of antiquity—at least potentially. But there was too much of the artist in him—he had no notion of laborious experiments, of trying to see things as they are—and those very qualities which still fascinate so many, his imagination and his artistic feeling, were in reality what prevented him from advancing in science. One line of Milton sums up at once his charm and his defect:

The next to fabling fell and smooth conceits.

Strange contrast that the man who banished arts should be the man in whom the spirit of arts stifled science!

In Plato everything, to use a chemical metaphor, is held in solution; by his greatest pupil and antagonist all the different elements were precipitated. What had formerly jostled together and interfered with one another, were now separated apart. A great deal of Aristotle's activity in ethics, politics, metaphysics, consisted in little but sifting and arranging what is to be found already in Plato. He had the genius of pigeon-holing, and he carries out the process remorselessly. At the same time he added much of his own, and especially he corrected or cut down the errors and superfluities into which Plato's luxuriant imagination had led him, and he created logic. Thus philosophy, as we now understand it, in him becomes an ordered system and a very dry one, but he can in no way be considered its creator except in logic—but the other part of philosophy as then understood, that is to say, aesthetics and the sciences apart from mathematics, were absolutely created by him.

Before speaking of Aristotle's achievements in this connexion one must make a distinction to be carefully kept in view. Aristotle may be reasonably taken to be the true patron of all University education in this respect—the Master of those who know, as Dante calls him—that he first disentangled and made plain the relative value of the sciences, art and philosophy. But he did not claim that all these should be represented in the actual education of the young—or of anybody. It is a great misfortune that most of his scheme of education is lost—perhaps it was never entirely completed. But we know enough of it to know that it was very like that of Plato in many ways. He was even stricter than Plato in his regulations about the sort of music which the young should study. He does not appear to have gone very much further in the allowance of poetry which he doled out. What he would have proposed about science and philosophy we simply do not know. A general education to be applied to all his free citizens was in fact still a comparatively small affair, and the notion of anything resembling a modern University never entered his head.

If he had resembled modern writers on the subject, he would have insisted that whatever interested *him* personally should be crammed down the throat of everybody else. But he was far from saying any such thing. And indeed when a man is interested, as *he* was, in every conceivable branch of knowledge, he is naturally preserved from such a desire. Of course, however, he never could, any more than any reasonable man, have contemplated any sort of education without Greek.

Nevertheless one may well admire in him that feature also, that in laying down a scheme of education he was absolutely devoid of any partiality or predilection for his own pursuits. Here again he went far beyond Plato—far beyond any other educationist with whom I am acquainted.

Secondly if he and Plato were practically agreed about education for the young, for people up to about eighteen or twenty, they differ *toto caelo* about what studies may be pursued in more advanced years. Plato, being first and foremost a metaphysician with a sort of religious system, would not have us study anything but metaphysics and a kind of mystic religion. But Aristotle, though his statements if he ever made any on this point are lost, plainly had no narrow views of that sort. He spent his life in research and teaching in almost every realm of knowledge then open, or then first conquered by him. He carried on, we may say, all by himself the whole business of both the Faculties of arts and science, creating many of his own subjects. Compared with him indeed what are any of us? ἐπάμεροι· τί δέ τις; τί δ' οὔτις; He was the greatest teacher and researcher of his time in aesthetics, ethics, logic, psychology, metaphysics, rhetoric, political science, political economy, constitutional history, theology, botany, zoology, embryology, anatomy, physiology, physics—I hope I have omitted none but am by no means sure—and in several of these his is the greatest name on record. Certainly here we have our two Faculties pretty well represented. The worst of it was that when he died no Committee under Heaven could have elected a Professor to succeed him.

To discuss Aristotle's scientific greatness in the very flimsiest manner, to narrate his achievements and estimate his position in science, would require a whole series of lectures—and it may be added that it would require somebody who knew something about it to deliver them. I must here content myself with quoting a testimony or two from those who are competent to speak. The late Dr Romanes, after reviewing Aristotle's work on biology, declares at the end that considered simply as a scientific man, to say nothing of his other writings, Aristotle is the greatest intellect the world has ever seen. When Ogle sent to Darwin his translation of Aristotle *On the Parts of Animals*, Darwin replied in these words in the course of his letter of acknowledgment:

From quotations which I had seen, I had a high notion

of Aristotle's merits, but I had not the most remote notion what a wonderful man he was. Linnaeus and Cuvier have been my two gods, though in very different ways, but they were mere schoolboys to old Aristotle.

George Henry Lewes wrote a book upon Aristotle, with the express purpose of denying and running down his scientific work. Martin Luther was fond of talking about devils and a great authority upon them (we all know how he once threw a bottle of ink) and he ought to know, if anybody ought to know, and *he* said that Aristotle was unquestionably a devil of the most malignant type; something of the same spirit animates Lewes' amiable book. Yet when he comes to the treatise *On the Generation of Animals*, by which embryology was founded, Lewes himself is melted, his hard heart is like the rock struck by Moses and gushes forth thus:

It is an extraordinary production. No ancient and few modern books equal it in comprehensiveness of detail and profound speculative insight. We there find some of the obscurest problems of Biology treated with a mastery which, when we consider the condition of science at that day, is truly astounding....I should not be candid were I to conceal the impression which the study of this work left on my mind, that the labours of the last two centuries have furnished the data to confirm many of the views of this prescient genius. Indeed I know no better eulogy to pass on Aristotle than to compare his work with the *Exercitations Concerning Generation* of our immortal Harvey. The founder of modern physiology was a man of keen insight, of patient research, of eminently scientific mind. His work is superior to that of Aristotle in some few anatomical details; but *it is so inferior to it in philosophy that at the present day it is much more antiquated, much less accordant with our views.*

That is pretty well, I think, for a hostile witness.

Such is the position Aristotle holds in science, and the Faculty of science should inscribe his name in letters of gold over their doors—what then did *he* think of the Faculty of arts? Did he, like his master, reject art and poetry and cast it forth into outer darkness? On the contrary, he appears as mediator between the two. Even as he stripped philosophy and science of the poetic glamour with which Plato had clothed them, and thereby put them into the right track, so he also stripped poetry of the false claims put forward by her admirers and cut away the ground of the objections taken by her opponents. It is not the business of poetry, he proclaimed, to teach ethics or politics. It is not the business of her critics to examine Homer's morality; let them neither exalt it into a rule of life, nor imagine it to be mischievous, for rightly understood it is neither the one nor the other. Poetry is concerned with the emotions, philosophy and science with the intellect. Both are needed to cultivate fully the double nature of man.

His treatise on poetry is the first and to this day the greatest on the subject. Dry indeed it is, but yet what else can such a work be? It is not the business of education to be amusing. Lessing declared it to be as infallible as Euclid, and Euclid seldom smiles.

Aristotle says himself: "Education ought certainly not to be turned into a means of amusement; for young people are not playing when they are learning, since all learning is accompanied with pain."

The study of literature, if it is to be of any good to us, must be serious. Reading *bad* novels is a pursuit precisely on a level with fancy needlework—both serve to fill up time—novels indeed have one advantage, they cannot be hung upon the backs of chairs. Since Aristotle's time the study of literature, considered as *mental* education and not only moral, has become of vastly more importance—it has become the study of foreign languages, dead or alive. It has itself become to a certain extent a sort of science, and it is in a scientific way that it must be treated in Colleges and Universities.

So science has gradually laid her hands upon everything, as far as teaching goes, and it was Aristotle who really began the process. It was he who made philosophy scientific by the introduction of a strict logic, and it was he who made the arts scientific by applying as scientific a method as possible to poetry. Education began by being nothing but art—Plato rejected art almost altogether and wanted to substitute a fanciful philosophy—Aristotle brought back art but made the treatment of it scientific.

The Middle Ages indeed reverted without knowing it to Platonism to a large extent. They thought themselves Aristotelians, but their new Faculty of Theology, the only important one with them, was the recrudescence in another form of the spirit of Platonic philosophy oddly bound and fettered by Aristotelian logic. Science could not move an inch, and arts were made the handmaid of the dominant theology. But with the great reformation of thought which made a new world in the sixteenth century the Aristotelian principles again got the upper hand in time. Yet the great revolt against the Middle Ages, which includes Protestantism and the Renaissance of Art and Science everywhere, made a dead set against Aristotle. His thought and doctrine held such sway over the mind of the whole world of Christendom that when it struggled to get out of its prison it thought Aristotle was its jailor. As Luther reckoned *him* along with the Pope to be the great enemy of religion and denounced him in that sweet language characteristic of him, so Galileo and Bacon took him for the great enemy of science! The foolish people whom Galileo had to vanquish were the blind followers of Aristotle, which is a very different story. Galileo was once present when a Venetian anatomist demonstrated that the origin of the nerves was the brain and not the heart and then asked an Aristotelian what he had to say. The philosopher after a pause replied: "You have made this appear so openly to my senses that I must needs confess it to be true *if it were not opposed by the text of Aristotle*, which says distinctly that the nerves spring from the heart." (As a matter of fact Aristotle never did say anything of the kind—but that is what comes of neglecting Greek.) But after these blind followers had been disposed of, the more that every branch of knowledge has advanced, the more has Aristotle been regarded as truly great and the more deeply has he been studied.

The great danger indeed of arts in Universities is nowadays that they are likely to be *too* scientific. The mere teaching of languages especially, continually tends to devour the enjoyment of them. It is pitiable to see people engaged in learning one grammar after another and cramming one set of idioms after another, and leaving the masterpieces of literature, to which these are the keys, unentered and untrod. A German philologist, being asked at the end of his life what he saw in Homer, answered scornfully *Roots*. And in truth philology is the curse of all our modern teaching of languages. The student of languages who neglects the literature is like the man Bunyan saw in the *Pilgrim's Progress*, occupied with a muck-rake, toiling in the dirt while all heaven opened its beauties above him and he saw them not. The wisest of the moderns bids us live in the Whole, the True, the Beautiful. The natural man is too prone to seek only the Beautiful, education is too prone to make us seek only the True in too limited a sense; let all so far as in us lies seek the Whole.

But a verse of Wordsworth even now occurs to me:

> Enough of science and of art—
>   close up these barren leaves.

EDWARD FITZGERALD

(Literary Society, University College, 1896)

Edward FitzGerald

Mr President, Ladies and Gentlemen,

When I was enticed into promising to read a paper before this learned Society, I pondered a good deal the question what subject or author to bring before you. And I concluded that if I could bring some of you acquainted with an author you might not know and who was very much worth knowing, I should be doing a greater service to you than by any amount of talking about people you know already.

No author seemed to me so fit for the purpose from this point of view as Edward FitzGerald. Though his great work has been before the world nearly forty years, and though he numbers more admirers every year, he is yet not generally known in the way that Tennyson, and Browning, and Swinburne are. At least, I think not. There is no reasonably cheap edition of him to be had, which is at once proof of this, and partly the cause of it, and several persons of my acquaintance have enrolled themselves my debtors for life for introducing him to them.

FitzGerald was born in 1809—an easy date to remember, for nearly everybody was born in 1809—I need only mention Tennyson and Darwin. His great work was published in 1859, the year of the *Origin of Species*. He died in 1883. Really, that is about all that anyone need want to know about his life until they know the man, and then they may want to know everything—*everything*. For the greater part of those seventy-four years he lived like a recluse in Suffolk, on the coast of the North Sea, dreaming his life away among dreams and shadows, except for his love of sailing—in *that* he was a true Briton. All the summer he used to be sailing about the east coast. Once he even went as far as Holland—to see Paul Potter's *Bull,* said a story about him, but, finding a fair wind back to England when he got there, he thought it a pity to lose it, and promptly sailed back without seeing Paul Potter or anything else. For the fishermen and sailors he had a great affection—in particular for one of them whom he made captain of his crew, and whom he called by the euphonious title of *Posh.* His real name is unrecorded. This Posh, said he, is one of the three greatest *Men* I have known—the other two being Tennyson and Thackeray—and Posh was superior to *them* in being less self-conscious. His morality, he says again, was that of Carlyle's heroes, the Norse sea-kings and people, not ours but different, and none the worse for that. Unluckily, one feature of Posh's morality was an ill-regulated thirst, and, after many remonstrances and broken vows, FitzGerald had to part company with him.

But it is not with the yachtsman but with the dreamer of dreams that we have to do here. For he dreamed *one* dream that is more lasting than we ourselves, or he, or the roses he planted, or the very Suffolk coast he lived on, which the sea is devouring by square miles every winter. Let us come to his great work. O, do not be afraid, I am not going to
> inflict again
> More books of blank upon the sons of men.

It is not an epic nor an essay on the character of Hamlet—

it is just 404 lines long, and very likely some of you know it all by heart already. And not only is it lamentably short, but it is only a translation. Yes, but what a translation! "a planet equal to the sun which cast it," says Tennyson of it.

There was born in Persia, in the latter half of the eleventh century, a certain Omar. He was a great man among the Persians, famous for learning, especially astronomy, and poetry and heterodoxy. He was one of the eight wise men who reformed the calendar, he was author of astronomical tables, and of a treatise on the extraction of cubic roots, and another on algebra, which he wrote in Arabic, as if it was not bad enough without. Probably no other man ever made the rebellious muse of mathematics (mad Mathesis, as Pope calls her) run so well in harness with her sister of verse. His poems consist simply of quatrains, little epigrams of four lines long a-piece; they are arranged in alphabetical order, and to read them in the original must be almost as festive as reading through a dictionary. Their subjects are—he was a Persian, and so, of course, his subjects are "praise of love and wine," and speculation in religious metaphysics. That is what *all* Persian poetry is, at least all the poetry of the great Persian poets, as far as I know, with one great exception. The passion of that nation for the nebulous, hazy region, which is not exactly philosophy because it is not logical, nor exactly religion because it is not practical, nor ethics because it is not dull—this passion of theirs, I say, is truly remarkable. Read Mr E. G. Browne's *A Year amongst the Persians*, and you will find them still at it to this day—they will not talk of anything else. They look at this world through a rosy

haze of mysticism, in which all things flow into one another
and nothing is plain, in which everything is a symbol of
something else, and, in the end, all things are absorbed in
the Divinity. More especially is it the great end of man to
get rid of his own individuality, and be mystically united
with God. This world is a mere illusion and a miserable
fraud—we must get rid of all desire, all passion, we must
remorselessly crush our own individuality—just as with the
Buddhists on the East and Stoics on the West. For until
we lose ourselves and *become* God, we cannot find ourselves.
This theory is most beautifully illustrated by a saying of
Jelaluddin: "One came to the Beloved's door (i.e. God),
and knocked. And a voice from within said: 'Who is there?'
And he said, 'It is I.' Then the voice said: 'This House will
not hold Me and Thee'; and the door was not opened unto
him. And the lover (the soul of man) departed into the
wilderness, and fasted and prayed in solitude. And after
a year he came again to the Beloved's door, and knocked.
And a voice from within said: 'Who is there?' and he said,
'It is THYSELF.' And the door was opened unto him."

Such is the region in which the Persian mind loves to
dwell, such the order of ideas amid which Omar grew up.
But there *he* could not stay. As he says himself:

> Myself when young did eagerly frequent
> Doctor and Saint, and heard great argument
>   About it and about; but evermore
> Came out by the same door where in I went.

> With them the seed of Wisdom did I sow,
> And with mine own hand wrought to make it grow;
>   And this was all the Harvest that I reaped—
> "I came like Water, and like Wind I go."

And he goes on, alluding to his astronomical studies:

Up from Earth's Centre, through the Seventh Gate,
I rose, and on the Throne of Saturn sate,
    And many a Knot unravelled by the Road,
But not the Master-knot of Human Fate.

There was the Door to which I found no Key,
There was the Veil through which I might not see:
    Some little talk awhile of ME and THEE,
There was—and then no more of THEE and ME.

So, failing to find any world but this, and any providence but destiny, he set about making the best of this world— in fact, he is not a romantic Stoic masquerading in a peacock's plumage, like his poetic brethren, but an Epicurean. The way in which he enforces the Epicurean view is, of course, principally by praising wine; for he is a Persian poet and a Mohammedan, to whom wine is forbidden by his religion. So it adds a piquancy to it, because it is naughty as well as nice. And, of course, the orthodox looked upon him with horror, though he was protected by the Sultan. So he says:

Indeed, the Idols I have loved so long
Have done my credit in this World much wrong;
    Have drowned my Glory in a shallow Cup,
And sold my Reputation for a Song.

Indeed, indeed, Repentance oft before,
I swore—but was I sober when I swore?
    And then and then came Spring, and Rose-in-hand
My threadbare Penitence apieces tore.

And much as Wine has played the Infidel,
And robbed me of my Robe of Honour—well,
    I wonder often what the Vintners buy
One half so precious as the stuff they sell.

And, in particular, he rebels against the doctrine of self-denial, which was universally preached by the Sufis, and which was inculcated in respect to wine by the Mohammedan religion—so wine with Omar is a type of the enjoyment of this world in general. Like Faust, he revolts against the command: "Entbehren sollst du, sollst entbehren—Das ist der ewige Gesang."—"What will you get?" asks the old sceptic; "The future life and all your mysticism are dreams—take what you can get *here*."

> I must abjure the Balm of Life, I must,
> Scared by some After-reckoning ta'en on trust,
> Or lured with Hope of some Diviner Drink,
> To fill the Cup—when crumbled into Dust!

> Oh threats of Hell and Hopes of Paradise!
> One thing at least is certain—*This* life flies;
> One thing is certain and the rest is Lies;
> The Flower that once has blown for ever dies.

Well, this old heathen remained very much in the shade for some eight hundred years, because of his unorthodoxy, and his alphabetical arrangement, and one thing or another, until he fell into the hands of FitzGerald, who, says Mr Swinburne, has made Omar one of the greatest of English poets. FitzGerald began studying Persian in 1853, under the guidance of Professor Cowell. He presently began turning odd stanzas of Omar into English—many into rhymed monkish Latin, too. And after a while he strung them together into a kind of chain with some connexion, and so made a sort of soliloquy in a garden out of the scattered jewels of Omar.

Persian scholars will tell one that FitzGerald palmed off a very inferior article on the English market; that he dressed up his Omar out of all recognition, making him appear taller than he really was, as Xenophon says of those Athenian ladies who had a strange custom of wearing high-heeled shoes. And they are quite indignant about it, looking upon us admirers of Omar just as we look on the benighted inhabitants of Continental Europe who persist in admiring Lord Byron long after *we* have exploded him. But, for all that, it appears that Omar really did strike FitzGerald as the most interesting of the Persian poets. It was just because he felt a certain kinship with him that he was able to make such a success out of him. For Fitz-Gerald wandered in the same valley of darkness himself. He, too, was naturally of a religious turn of mind; on his tomb are inscribed, by his own wish, the words: "It is He that has made us, and not we ourselves," and yet he, too, failed to find any world but this. In Omar he could find that same idea of resignation to that which "has made us and not we ourselves," just as in Aeschylus or Marcus Aurelius, or the greatest of all poems that deal with these mysteries—the Book of *Job*. For has not Omar said:

> We are no other than a moving row
> Of Magic Shadow-shapes that come and go—
>   Round with the Sun-illumined Lantern held
> In Midnight by the Master of the show;

> But helpless Pieces of the Game He plays
> Upon this Chequer-board of Nights and Days;
>   Hither and thither moves, and checks, and slays,
> And one by one back in the Closet lays.

> The Ball no question makes of Ayes and Noes,
> But Here or There as strikes the Player goes;
>   And He that tossed you down into the Field,
> *He* knows about it all—HE knows—HE knows!

The Moving Finger writes; and, having writ,
Moves on: nor all your Piety nor Wit
  Shall lure it back to cancel half a Line,
Nor all your Tears wash out a Word of it.

Ah, make the most of what we yet may spend,
Before we too into the Dust descend;
  Dust into Dust, and under Dust to lie
Sans Wine, sans Song, sans Singer, and—sans End!

It is not a lofty or heroic strain, no doubt; many persons are sure always to be shocked by it, and to say that it is nothing but the despairing cry: "Let us eat and drink, for to-morrow we die." "I know you will thank me," writes FitzGerald to a friend, when sending him a copy, "and I think you will feel a sort of 'triste Plaisir' in it, as others besides myself have felt. It is a desperate sort of thing, unfortunately at the bottom of all thinking men's minds; but made music of." In those words he exhausts all criticism of his own poem. Never, surely, did any poet more justly weigh his own work in a single sentence.

But FitzGerald's way of making the best of this world was very different from the easy Epicurean philosophy which Omar professed, and which he appears to have, to some extent, practised. Assuredly Omar was no vulgar Epicurean himself—he, who was qualified to be a professor of mathematics—but, for all that, the burden of his song is simply:

Drink!—for, once dead, you never shall return.

Strange, indeed, that such a doctrine should be popularised in England by the man whose motto was Plain Living and High Thinking, the man who would give his friends of the best when they came to see him, while he himself would walk up and down the room, munching an apple or a turnip. I am not inventing; his biographer *says* a *turnip*. For he was a vegetarian—indeed, he once nearly killed Tennyson, by persuading him, too, to turn vegetarian for six weeks.

Well, you have a pretty good idea by this time of the contents and of the style of the poem. Now for a word on FitzGerald's principles of translation. The unhappy translator is always being impaled on the horns of a dilemma. If he translates literally, he produces stuff no mortal can read. "I am sure," says FitzGerald elsewhere of another poem, "I am sure a complete translation, even in prose, would not have been a *readable* one, which, after all, is a useful property of most books, *even of poetry.*" If, on the other hand, he makes a good and readable thing of it, then arise all the people who know the original, and begin to peck at it like domestic fowl. If one steers a middle course, one pleases nobody. FitzGerald boldly adopted the principle that what is wanted in a translation is *this*: To give people who don't know the original a sort of idea of the effect it produces on people who do. For this end we must throw all attempt at a *literal* translation to the wind. We must soak ourselves in the spirit of an author, and reproduce that spirit in as good poetic style as we may be master of. So, not only with Omar, but with his other translations too, he omits whole passages, puts in bits of his own, modifies and arranges everything, and makes— a poem. It is interesting to compare Paley's translation of the *Agamemnon* of Aeschylus with FitzGerald's from this point of view. Paley assures us himself, in his preface (and I suppose he ought to know), that *his* is readable and tolerably literal, and then offers us such gems as: "You are some crazy-headed person, or possessed by some god"; or, again, "And my inward parts do not vainly bode—the heart that whirls in eddies against the midriff, while it justly looks for a fulfilment of its fears." Really, if Aeschylus is that sort of thing, why do we rise up early and so late take rest that we may proceed B.A. in Arts? Now listen to another bit from FitzGerald, about Helen's flight from Menelaus:

Not beside thee in the chamber,
Menelaus, any more;
But with him she fled with, pillow'd,
On the summer softly-billow'd
Ocean, into dimple wreathing
Underneath a breeze of amber
Air that, as from Eros breathing,
Fill'd the sail and flew before;
Floating on the summer seas,
Like some sweet Effigies
Of Eirène's self, or sweeter
Aphrodite, sweeter still:
With the Shepherd, from whose luckless
Hand upon the Phrygian hill
Of the three Immortals, She
The fatal prize of Beauty bore,
Floating with him o'er the foam
She rose from, to the shepherd's home
On the Ionian shore.

There is hardly a word, hardly a single word of all that in Aeschylus. But which of the two gives one the impression that Aeschylus gives—Paley or FitzGerald?

But, of course, FitzGerald could not escape the domestic fowl. Just listen to one of them cackling. The most

splendid stanzas of the whole poem are those which end
the first long soliloquy:

> O Thou, who didst with Pitfall and with Gin
> Beset the Road I was to wander in,
>   Thou wilt not with Predestination round
> Enmesh, and then impute my Fall to Sin!

> O Thou, who Man of baser Earth didst make,
> And even with Paradise devise the Snake;
>   For all the Sin wherewith the Face of Man
> Is blackened, Man's forgiveness give—and take!

By the addition of the last two words, FitzGerald has
turned a commonplace idea enough into the most fearful
indictment ever uttered by Man against his Maker. One
would have thought that any comment on it could only take
the form of admiration. But Professor Cowell—well, Professor Cowell is a Professor, and I do not like to hear
persons of dignity lightly spoken of, and, moreover, he was
a good friend to FitzGerald as ever man had, and it is
thanks to him that he ever learnt any Persian at all, and
that we are talking about him here to-day—*but*, I say,
Cowell writes: "There is no original for the line about the
snake" (as if anybody cared); "I have looked for it in vain
in Nicholas; but I have always supposed that the last line
is FitzGerald's *mistaken version* of Quatrain 236. Fitz-
Gerald mistook the meaning of *giving* and *accepting* as used
here, and so invented his last line *out of his own mistake*.
I wrote to him about it when I was in Calcutta, but he
never cared to alter it." He never cared to alter it! The
unconscious irony in those last words is simply delicious.
And how characteristic of FitzGerald is the story. Any
other man, one would think, would have written back to

consign the Professor to a hotter climate than Calcutta,
and to observe that, if there was any one line in the
English language a man might be proud of, it was just
that. But FitzGerald was the most modest of men, "one
who as persistently avoided fame as others seek it." I can
fancy him smiling over that remonstrance, and putting off
his corrector, giving him the impression that he (Cowell)
was quite right, but that his poor verses were really not
worth troubling about.

Well, let us thank the gods that *we* know no Persian, and
try to estimate the position of this Omar purely as *English*
literature. I always think of Gray's *Elegy* in connexion
with it. "And Gray," says FitzGerald, in one of his letters,
"ah, to think of that little Elegy inscribed among the
stars, while —— & Co. are blazing away with their fireworks here on earth." Even so did he himself inscribe that
little elegy of his among the stars, while nobody heard or
thought about him, and while all the literary papers were
full of those other noisy people. Not that I fail myself to
like them, but it certainly is my opinion that FitzGerald
may very likely outlast the whole gang of them, just as
Gray's *Elegy* has beaten all the works of his contemporaries,
who were so much more brilliant than he. Each of the two
lived more or less in seclusion, buried with their books—
the world forgetting, by the world forgot—each polished
his little elegy for years. The subject of each is very much
the same—quite commonplace—nothing out of the way,
just such reflections as every man makes about life and
death, and, therefore, as immortal in essence as man himself.
Whatever creeds may rise and fall, whatever mutabilities
of empire and science and manners there may be, so long

as we are, in the end of it all these reflections must strike home.

> The boast of heraldry, the pomp of power,
> And all that beauty, all that wealth e'er gave,
> Awaits alike the inevitable hour....

Each of the two was so fastidious that he rejected at least one of the most beautiful stanzas, now to be found only in the notes.

On a close comparison, I think—I am afraid—the palm must be yielded to Gray. His *Elegy* is better arranged as a whole—naturally, when one thinks how the other was pieced together out of the chaotic heap of the original Omar. And taking stanza for stanza, line for line, there are better stanzas and better lines in Gray. He has not the same natural easy flow as FitzGerald, whether melancholy or humorous or whimsical, but he has more weight and dignity and power. He took himself more seriously. Modesty is a good thing, or so they say who understand about it, but FitzGerald was perhaps *too* modest; if he had been more ambitious he might have taken even more pains than he did, and insisted deliberately on making a treasure for ever, as Gray did. Yet, perhaps he would have spoilt it, so we had better be content. Then, too, when we compare the two, we must allow for the lapse of time. Time has laid a decaying finger here and there upon Gray. There are bits of the *Elegy* which are written in the poetic slang of the day; "Froze the genial current of the soul," for example, is as detestable a piece of eighteenth-century poetic slang as you can find; such things pass muster well enough in their own time, when everybody is used to expressions of the sort, but after a while they turn out to be colours which will not last. And how do we know how much poetic slang of the *nineteenth* century there may not be in Fitz-Gerald? At any rate, as Omar has it, "One thing is certain, and the rest is Lies"—the Persian allusions in FitzGerald are a nuisance. One is always liable to an incursion of Oriental tinsel in European poetry. Goethe, Hugo, Leconte de Lisle, Byron, Bodenstedt, have all amused themselves with it and irritated us. And then there was Moore. When I was young, some forty years ago, people used still to read *Lalla Rookh*, and used to like to talk about Bendemeer's stream, and the Green Sea, and yataghans, and such a deal of skimble-skamble stuff. You could not read ten lines without looking at a note to find out what was meant by a *zel* or a *chibouk* or a *talipot tree*; things about which Moore knew no more than I do; but which he had laboriously crammed up in Oriental dictionaries. These things, too, are of the nature of fireworks, and, though they may take the fancy for a time, they soon lose all their lustre. "I do not like the fashion of your garments," said King Lear to a person whose only "apparatus" was a blanket; "you will say, they are Persian, but let them be changed." That is a very appropriate motto for poetry of the kind.

> "Well, let it take them," says FitzGerald,
> "what have we to do
> With Kaikobád the Great or Kaikhosrú?"

A sentiment one often echoes. Only he did not deliberately drag them in. On the contrary, he cut quantities out. Still, in the long run, it must be a great advantage to Gray that he is purely English—or, rather, purely human, for even to England there is hardly an allusion in his *Elegy*.

Yet, surely, when all allowance is made for the effects of time, and the weariness of Persian allusion, such lines as these must be as "immortal," as we are pleased to call it, as Gray himself:

They say the Lion and the Lizard keep
The Courts where Jamshýd gloried and drank deep:
    And Bahrám, that great Hunter—the Wild Ass
Stamps o'er his Head, but cannot break his Sleep.

I sometimes think that never blows so red
The Rose as where some buried Cæsar bled;
    That every Hyacinth the Garden wears
Dropt in her Lap from some once lovely Head.

And this reviving Herb whose tender Green
Fledges the River-Lip on which we lean—
    Ah lean upon it lightly! for who knows
From what once lovely Lip it springs unseen!

Ah, my Belovéd, fill the Cup that clears
To-DAY of past Regrets and future Fears:
    To-morrow!—Why, To-morrow I may be
Myself with Yesterday's Sev'n thousand Years.

For some we loved, the loveliest and the best
That from his Vintage rolling Time hath prest,
    Have drunk their Cup a Round or two before,
And one by one crept silently to rest.

"But time goes on, and shorter paths I know," says Pindar. FitzGerald made many other translations: *Salaman and Absal*, from Jami; *Bird-Parliament*, from Attar—Persians both. Both poems deal, of course, with the eternal mysticism, the abnegation of the body and union of the soul with God. I will read an extract from the *Bird-Parliament*, which is a fable to satirise those who hesitate between this world and the other:

There was a Queen of Egypt like the Bride
Of Night, Full-moon-faced and Canopus-eyed,
Whom one among the meanest of her Crowd
Loved—and she knew it, (for he loved aloud)
And sent for him, and said "Thou lov'st thy Queen:
Now therefore Thou hast this to choose between:
Fly for thy Life: or for this one night Wed
Thy Queen, and with the Sunrise lose thy Head."
He paused—he turned to fly—she struck him dead.
"For had he truly loved his Queen," said She,
"He would at once have given his Life for me,
And Life and Wife had carried: but he lied;
And loving only Life, has justly died."

He also translated the *Agamemnon* and both the *Oedipuses*, and eight plays of Calderon. But the British public *will not* swallow Calderon in any shape; I suppose he must be read in the original, and I daresay it would turn out that he is not worth the trouble. I should advise anyone who may be tempted to look at them to begin with the *Mighty Magician*. Then he made a boiled-down version of Crabbe's *Tales of the Hall*, which, I think, has never been published. Crabbe was a great passion of his, he was always trying to cram him down other people's throats. "Positively, I am at my eternal Crabbe again," he says, in a letter to Mrs Kemble. But it is no use; in the race for oblivion Crabbe has easily distanced even Hazlitt[1].

Then there is a prose dialogue called *Euphranor*, which, to *my* taste, seemed scarce worth reading, though Tennyson

[1] A paper in praise of Hazlitt had lately been read to the Society. Platt afterwards came to a better judgment of Crabbe.

called the end of it the finest piece of English prose he knew! So do tastes differ.

But what seems like to live best after Omar is the *Letters*—one series to different friends and another to Fanny Kemble. Which of the two is the more delightful I do not know; but I think there are no other letters like them in English. Pieces of delightful literary criticism— often fearfully unorthodox; but what a joy it is to meet a man who says what he thinks, and does not feel bound to admire what he doesn't admire. He deplores his own taste in the most simple manner, how he could not like Goethe, for instance, and how he could not read ten lines of *Paradise Lost* because of some pedantic classical allusion or construction, which "sends one from Hell or Heaven to the school-room, worse than either." "Well, but I believe in the Vox Populi of two hundred years; still more of two thousand," he writes; *he* would not set up his own private taste above the world's, as most of us are so fond of doing. Then there are most unexpected and capricious ideas always turning up. Thus of a sonata of Beethoven's he writes: "It is meant to express the discord and gradual atonement of two lovers, and Beethoven was disgusted that every one did not see what was meant; *in truth*, it expresses *any* resistance gradually overcome—Dobson shaving with a blunt razor, for instance." What other mortal would ever have compared a Beethoven sonata to a man shaving? Then his banter about Spedding, the editor and biographer of Bacon, and his own dearest friend. Spedding had an immense forehead, and was bald, like all truly great men, and FitzGerald tells us of drawings of Swiss lakes, with Spedding's forehead rising over the mountains; and, again, when Spedding went to America, we are gravely told of the confusion caused to the shipping in the Channel, because the sailors would mistake his forehead for Beachy Head.

But I hear two objections taken to the Letters—they are too feminine, and the Capital Letters are used in a chaotic way at the beginning of words. Well, the Capitals can be left alone. He always had a Fancy for Them; but, as to the other charge, is it not just that feminine quality which gives the Letters their charm? In a general of division or an anatomist or a New Woman to be feminine may be a mistake; but here what have we to do with that? One does not want a man to write letters in the spirit in which he would lead a charge of cavalry! It is just that feminine quality in his nature which makes the man himself and his letters so lovable. "One loves Virgil somehow," he says, after quoting him in one of them, and is it not just the same with Virgil, whom the Neapolitans nicknamed the Maid? It is that gentle melancholy temperament which gives its charm to the verse of both. The letters of Horace Walpole may be infinitely more brilliant and sparkling, they may have more amusing stories in them, but one does not love Walpole—not a bit.

It has been said of FitzGerald that he writes to his friends rather as a lover than as a friend. And he says himself in a letter of 1834:

Your letter has indeed been a long time coming, but it is all the more delicious. Perhaps you can't imagine how wistfully I have looked for it; how, after a walk, my eyes have turned to the table, on coming into the room, to see it. Sometimes I have been tempted to be angry with you; but then I thought that I was sure you would come a hundred miles to serve me, though you were too lazy to sit down to a letter. I suppose that people who are engaged in serious ways of life, and are of well-filled minds, don't think much about the interchange of letters with any anxiety; but I am an idle fellow, of a very ladylike turn of sentiment, and my friendships are more like loves, I think.

Therefore perhaps it was that he was so much beloved by those who knew. Tennyson and Thackeray both counted him the dearest of all their friends, and so, no doubt, did the Third Great Man, Posh. Even Carlyle, who had a good word for nobody, could find nothing to say against him worse than to call him "the ultra-modest man, with his peaceable, far-niente life." Of course, Carlyle would have no sympathy with his pursuits; to translate Persian and Greek and Calderon was, in the language of the philosopher, to occupy one's self with dead dogs. "Unser Zeitalter bedarf kräftiger Geister," said a greater than Carlyle, and yet at odd times, despite Presidents and Kaisers, one may still dream with a melancholy pleasure over that eternal lamentation, old as the song of Linus among the cornfields, or the wailing of the Syrian maidens over their wounded Thammuz:

Yet Ah, that Spring should vanish with the Rose!
That Youth's sweet-scented Manuscript should close!
    The Nightingale that in the branches sang,
Ah whence, and whither flown again, who knows!

But, to borrow a phrase from an Alexandrine poet, the Nightingales of FitzGerald yet live, and shall sing to generations yet unborn when we are all with Kaikobád and Kaikhosrú.

ARISTOPHANES

(The Quarto, vol. IV, 1898)

Aristophanes

IT is one of those things which are generally known that Plato declared a truceless war upon the poets, and not only ejected Homer with the greatest respect indeed, but with stern decision, from his ideal polity, but also said that tragedy and comedy did a great deal more harm than good; and these opinions of his have been a good deal talked about because Plato is the chosen philosopher of all those who are by nature hopelessly unphilosophical, like you and me.

His objection to tragedy is briefly that it encourages you to weep and carry on about the misfortunes of imaginary characters in a way of which you would be ashamed in real life if a misfortune happened to yourself. The tendency of the natural man is to give way to his grief, but the philosopher ought to be stoical, and tragedy feeds the natural tendency and is therefore bad. Aristotle, who conceived his mission to be principally to set Plato right, and who did it with great energy and success, turned this very objection of Plato's with extraordinary skill into the justification of tragedy. The tendency to give way to misfortune, he answered, is a tendency which will grow in us if we do not get rid of it, just like a malignant humour in the body, and there is nothing better to be done than to purge it out of us. Tragedy enables us to get rid of it periodically, and the more we do so by a good cry occasionally over fictitious evils, the more shall we be able to resist real evils with the dignity befitting a student of moral science. It is an interesting circumstance that the Aristotelian view was first correctly understood by the great Milton, as may be seen from his preface to *Samson Agonistes*.

Plato's objection to comedy was of a similar nature. Comedy encourages you to laugh at things of which you would be ashamed in private life. And remember that the comedy of those days was a comedy of a licence and indecency and virulent personal abuse of living men to which no parallel has ever been seen since upon the stage[1]. Why, the old comedy shocked even the public, for it was put a stop to by the authorities in course of time. It is true that what shocked *them* was not the immorality and indecency, it was the free political criticism and the personal abuse, abuse which naturally fell principally on the authorities themselves. But when once its wings had been clipped, the old comedy languished like a bird in a cage, and soon died.

What did Aristotle answer here? or what would he have answered? It is not certain that he tried to justify the old comedy at all; he appears to have thought Menander, not Aristophanes, the true type of comedy. But we may at least answer on his own lines that just as tragedy was valuable as purging us of the natural tendency to lamentation, so the old comedy was valuable as purging us of the natural tendency to laugh at what we ought not, as civilised and rational beings, to laugh at at all. An occasional giving up of ourselves to the instinct of the unregenerate savage to rejoice in all manner of abominations will make us all the better able to play the part of members of a civilised, cultivated and polite society as a rule.

---

[1] By Plato's time the old comedy was already dead and buried, but if he objected so strongly to the middle comedy, *à fortiori* would he have objected to Aristophanes. (Author's note.)

But I daresay you are asking all this time why comedy or art of any kind should have *any* moral effect on people. Well, all I can say is that the Greek persistently looked upon it from that point of view. Art must be useful according to them, or it is nothing. And as they are the only people in the history of the world who ever had a genuine and natural feeling for art, and as they created every form of art in existence, they have some right to be heard. No doubt to say art must be useful is the most Philistine thing one well *can* say, but what is one to say of the modern doctrine which had such vogue in France in 1830 and onwards, the cry of "art for art," which has ended in Zola? If art exists for art, what has it to do with me? "Art for man" is the only rational doctrine for an artist who is a man himself. And that means that it must be useful? Well, I don't know; what do you mean by useful? Some people talk as if nothing were useful which one cannot eat or drink or run to death over a ploughed field in a scarlet coat. "The beautiful is as useful as the useful, even more useful," said Hugo, and I think he was right, and that the Greeks were right too.

But let us go back to the old comedy, to what is summed up for us in the one name Aristophanes, and apply some of all this "bald disjointed chat" to him. First of all let us look at the way Bergk opens his chapter on Attic comedy. It is, says he, a painting of manners, an imitation of ordinary life. At the same time he admits that Aristophanes is one of the greatest writers of comedy. Bless me, what a confusion of thought there stands revealed in the mere juxtaposition of these two sentences! If comedy is never anything but an imitation of life, Aristophanes is not only not a great writer of comedy, he is not a comic writer at all, he is the most incompetent and ridiculous of bunglers, and ought to be hissed off the stage. Why then is he a great writer of comedy? Because comedy, in its origin, was a literature of revolt against convention, and he has carried this revolt further than any other writer.

"Man," says The Philosopher, "is more gregarious than any beast of the field, yea, than any whatsoever of the social hymenoptera." But think what a price those poor hymenoptera pay for their society! The majority of them reduced to a neuter asexual condition, a swarm of males whose principal occupation is being massacred annually, a Royal Family exclusively employed in laying eggs! Happier surely the roving humble-bee, who lives like the Cyclops, "without society and without law, ruling over his wife and children, nor do they trouble themselves about one another." Imagine a hive-bee suddenly endowed with the speech, the insight, and the fun of an Aristophanes; what a new *Parliament of Bees* could he compose! Now in every man there is a humble-bee as well as a hive-bee; not only is he naturally gregarious, but he is also naturally an animal who seeks to gratify his passions as they come to him. And along with this he has developed moral, political, and social sentiments, which distinguish him from gorilla or tiger; nor only so, but "by policy and long process of time" he has agreed tacitly or avowedly to bind himself by a host of restrictions. There are laws engraved or engrossed on brass or iron or parchment, and there are laws innumerable not written anywhere, but practically recognised by everyone. The law "thou shalt not kill," or at least "thou shalt not kill a member of thy own tribe," is the most binding of all, for without it all society would fall to pieces. The law "thou shalt not tell thy neighbour what thou really thinkest of him" is equally binding in civilised society; whoso breaks it habitually will lose all his friends, unless he be as fortunate in them as I am. Then, again, it is a law that a man should wear a particular kind of dress (and what a dress!) in London, and hence the "Philosophy of Clothes" may be used to illustrate the true theory of the old comedy. For when we flee away for the summer we throw off this constraint with great joy, wear whatever seems comfortable, set all the dictates of decorum and etiquette at defiance. And a breach of custom of this kind does us all the good in the world; we return refreshed to the routine of London, and are able to keep it up without undue depression for another year. No doubt this is a very mild example, but it is on the same lines. As we revolt against many small conventionalities in our holidays, so the Athenians revolted in their comedies, at festivals like the Dionysia, in a far more thorough and energetic fashion. On these occasions all the instincts of the animal within us, which are repressed by society, were again wakened up.

And above the animal lies another stratum, that of the unthinking, unheroic, commonplace "homme sensuel moyen." He, too, is allowed his fling, when Strepsiades triumphs over Socrates, or Sganarelle over philosopher and physician. The virulent abuse of people we do not like finds here its vent; indeed, comedy is said to have arisen from the custom of merrymakers abusing one another in extempore Billingsgate on the Bank Holidays of those days, and abuse of this sort remained a prominent feature in the full-blown art. When Dante had got a very long way down in hell, he stopped listening to a very unedifying quarrel between Messer Adamo of Brescia and the Greek Sinon. Virgil, who represents the Reason, rebukes him for it, and tells him that if he listen any longer he will be angry with him, and Dante, with great shame, leaves them to their quarrel and passes on. This natural and low instinct in us which leads us to be amused at hearing two people abuse one another, whether in the street, in the pit of hell, or the pages of *Nature*, was indulged to the height. Especially in politics the abuse of prominent statesmen, which even now reaches a considerable pitch in the evening papers, was carried to prodigious lengths, and in the most vulgar style. The whole political system is part of our conventionality, it is irksome to the natural man, and he likes now and then to rise and declaim against it though he really knows it to be necessary. The unrestricted freedom of speech in its lower forms is one of the most prominent features of the old comedy; society makes us restrain our instinct to say what we think of people and things we do not like, and put things mildly, and comedy did away with this restraint.

Then there is the revolt against morality as a whole. In every respect the natural instinct prevails. To lie, to steal, to kill, if it suits your purpose, is the natural thing to do in the old comedy. If any danger threatens, you run away. Hence the typical hero is a coward and an immoral rascal, if you look at him seriously. The most prominent feature of this revolt against morality was the incredible indecency of these representations, to which there was absolutely no limit.

Moreover religion fettered the Greek continually, a splendid glittering pompous religion, all external without a scrap of genuine inward religious feeling. To connect it with morality was left to a few poets and philosophers; to the general public it was ritual, combined with a ridiculous mythology. But this ritual was a very serious matter, it came into everything one did. Sacrifices and libations, and an eternal round of religious festivals—even tragedy and comedy were religious ceremonies—hampered the Athenian at every turn. Hence naturally we find the revolt against religion along with the rest, and those gods who were worshipped by the state, and for disbelieving in whom (as his accusers said) the wisest and best of the Athenians was put to death, these very gods are brought on the stage under every circumstance of ridicule and buffoonery. And that too by the very man who attacked Socrates in another play for his alleged "atheism"! This shews pretty clearly how unsafe it is to argue from the plays of Aristophanes to his real sentiments.

Lastly—or at least the last thing I shall here remark on—the natural man rises up in all his glory as a punster. There is perhaps nothing more disgusting to his neighbours. The man who whistles, the man who is in love, the man who talks football shop, the man who runs college magazines—all of these pale their ineffectual fires before him. Yet there is nothing more natural to man than to make puns, children revel in the most idiotic, the stone age I conceive was worse plagued with them than with any other curse of primitive man, and *Pithecanthropus erectus*, if he was able to talk at all, punned like a Lamb. Only a long and severe course of civilisation has checked them, and even now they are not as extinct as might be wished. In Aristophanes they appear in all their native hideousness, "naked and not ashamed" like the rest of him. Nothing annoys one so much in him now as these silly puns; presumably they pleased at the time, but in that respect at any rate we may boast that our comic taste has improved since.

Yet all this revolt against constraint and civilisation has nothing bitter about it; it is always perfectly good-humoured in spite of the satire which pervades and permeates it, and finds vent not in sneers but in open gigantic laughter. Often enough has it been seen that a great man has been disgusted by the falsehoods and hypocrisy which are in some degree necessary to society—only lately a very little man named Nordau has been holding forth about them— or by the lower animal which is the substratum of the human creature. Neither the one nor the other can be helped; society cannot exist without shams, and man cannot become an angel all at once. The wise and healthy mind will recognise this and make the best of it. But certain minds fix themselves upon the wrong side of the tapestry; they become embittered in consequence, and find vent in a satire which is not good-humoured but savage, not Aristophanic but—who has not already thought of the dreadful name of Swift? To him all the disagreeable part of life which we keep dark became so prominent, and so tortured his sensitive spirit that he could think of no- thing else; hence rose like a Fury from the pit that "saeva indignatio" which lacerated a heart surely by nature lovable and noble, till it turned him into the most tremendous satirist the world has ever seen. Whoever reads the last voyage of Gulliver may well feel unclean

4-2

until the evening and for many days. Like the old comedy, Swift cuts off from man all his nobler growth, and displays the ghastly skeleton beneath him, but instead of being a wholesome draught his comedy has become as the waters of Marah. Neither representation of man is true, but Swift pretends that his is so, and the horror of it is that he makes his reader think so too.

In Rousseau the revolt takes a diametrically opposite form. He says that civilisation is a bad thing, and we ought to return to the happy state of things "when wild in woods the noble savage ran." If he had only known as much of savages as we do! But here we meet a philosophical theory, not literature. Such theories were familiar enough at Athens also.

A greater name by far than these will give us another example. There was a period in Shakespeare's life when that milk of human kindness which was so sweet in him, turned sour, when he wrote satire as bitter and almost as terrible as Swift's; *why*, we cannot tell, for no hand will lift the curtain that veils his inner life. It was the period of *Lear, Timon, Troilus*. But his divine nature righted itself again, and in his latest plays came back a serenity and sweetness all the more heavenly for the storm he had passed through.

> If after every tempest come such calms
> May the winds blow till they have wakened death;

but I know of no parallel in literature. Dante's bitterest satire is uttered in the heaven of heavens.

All general and wide satire thus springs from the same root in our nature as does the earliest comedy. But the professional satirists, hideous owls like Juvenal, who screech in a night without moon or star, are a brood not to be mentioned in connexion with such good company. They are to comedy as vinegar to wine, and they are not even sincere as Swift was. When satire informs and invigorates the comedy of manners, the later comedy which really *is* an imitation of life, then, indeed, we come to something of the same kind and to the one writer of comic drama[1] who is truly worthy to be set beside Aristophanes, "Molière, ce moqueur grave comme un apôtre." Yet what a difference! that line of Hugo's is as admirable as a description of Molière as it would be absurd if applied to the other. In Molière the satire is indeed grave and serious; with all his unsurpassed comic power his greatest works are almost like tragedies in tone and impression; and then the revolt in him is not against all society but only against court follies and aristocratic manners[2]. Yet what he loses in width, he makes up for again in other ways, in the magnificent characterisation, in the common sense which goes beyond the flights of mere poetry as the common sense of Socrates did beyond the flights of Plato, in that depth of feeling and restrained passion which positively sometimes

[1] The romantic comedy is here excluded as being altogether of a different type. *Twelfth Night* and *Amor Honor y Poder* and *La Boba para los Otros*, Hugo's *Esca*, and Musset's *Fantasio* may be a more delightful species of literature than anything else in existence, but strictly speaking can hardly be ranked as "comedy" proper. (Author's note.)

[2] Of course this is only a single detail in Molière among many others. Revolt is not the essential principle with him. He is the culmination of the later comedy, and hence it is that he draws upon Plautus and Terence when he adapts a play from the ancients. What could he have got from Aristophanes to suit his peculiar bent? It is a curious thing that the only successful adaptation of Aristophanes should have been made by, of all people, the sweet, tender and sublime Racine. (Author's note.)

reminds one of Sophocles, as in the great scene of Agnès and Arnolphe, in that warfare upon cant and hypocrisy in which he again resembles Socrates and which makes some people so angry with him, in that power of treating an ethical subject all round from every point of view which makes *Le Misanthrope* so great—and so difficult to appreciate. Look at what Mr Morley says about this same *Misanthrope* in his book on Voltaire, how he is puzzled with it, how angry he gets with this prodigious mind which is so wide in its view, that it cannot take up one side against the other. In truth he evidently has a well-grounded suspicion that if Molière had known him he would have laughed consumedly at *him*, the Right Honourable John Morley. And Schlegel had the same uneasy feeling too; Schlegel is of course one of the very silliest persons who ever undertook to criticise literature; he had immense knowledge and no judgment, he understood as much about poetry as comparative philologists usually do, he was "no true man" said Goethe. Such a person in the presence of Molière blinks like an owl in the sun, and of all his absurd criticism that upon Molière is probably, to use a celebrated phrase of his own, "the very vilest."

However, the only modern writer in whom the genuine Aristophanic genius reappears is a man who did not write comedies—he could not have done it had he tried—a man whom it is hardly respectable to mention, Rabelais. One cannot recommend anybody to read him as a whole, for a great deal of him is really very dull, but everybody ought to know Besant's delightful *Readings in Rabelais*. But after all the difference is very great. He has the same outrageous laughter, the same revolt against all constraint—and natural enough in him was this revolt, for at nine years of age he was put into a monastery and all the joy of life cut off from him, and when he came out the rebound might be expected to be violent enough—but he was no Greek in spirit and had no sense of form, so that he often becomes utterly amorphous, the common snare of the humourist, and he had no lyric capacity. The "climbing apes" were there, but not the "singing nightingales," to quote the phrase of Heine concerning Aristophanes. Panurge is the one modern example of the typical character of the old comedy, but where is the song of the *Clouds* or of the *Birds*? And, moreover, the whole thing is not worked out with the unity and thoroughness of the ancients. The great and wise Pantagruel is a noble figure in himself in the later books, but he is out of place in his surroundings.

As I have referred to Heine's famous description, I will take this opportunity of observing that this revolt against convention is what Heine must have meant by his obscure phrase "world-annihilation." It is out of a "world-annihilation," he says, that springs the fantastic tree of Aristophanic comedy, with its climbing apes and singing nightingales. It means that Aristophanes first annihilates the *social* world and order in which we live, and then builds up his fantasies on the ground which remains, that is on the lower nature of man. This, too, is what Hegel was groping after when he talked of the "subjectivity" of comedy, which Mahaffy makes such fun of, and quite fairly. But they say that Hegel generally meant something if only you could find out what. Anyhow, this "subjectivity" is the individual rising up against society and everything outside him, and asserting his own will for the moment as the only law to be obeyed.

So far we have considered Attic comedy in its general aspect; now consider the particular circumstances in which Aristophanes found himself. He was an Athenian, shut up in the city by the exigencies of the war with Sparta. He lived when the new learning of the Sophists—which was like the criticism of the French *philosophes* in the last century—was overrunning Greece, and all the old beliefs, religious, moral, and social, were crumbling into chaos under that dissolving acid. He lived under a democracy, guided or humoured by statesmen of a type we know only too well in England.

Now the ordinary constraints of civilisation are nothing to the constraint imposed by the war on the Athenians. They lived a free and easy life on their estates and farms, they hated being cooped up in the city and having all their vines and fruit-trees and crops destroyed. Of course therefore the spirit of revolt shows itself in violent attacks upon the war and everybody concerned with it. Aristophanes is for ever preaching peace; it is the natural instinct to avoid trouble and disagreeables; the higher policy, Pericles and the statesmen, may insist on the necessity and the advantages of war, but the natural man submits to it with grumbling, and his grumbling finds a furious voice in comedy. The *Peace* is entirely devoted to it, and there is hardly a play in which it does not turn up somewhere. Dicaeopolis triumphing over Lamachus is the blissful vision which fancy substitutes for the melancholy truth. But did Aristophanes *really* think the war was wrong? Goodness only knows.

In just the same way, comedy must always attack the prevailing party in politics. Whatever party is in power, the people must feel themselves to some extent constrained by it; they will always be to some extent "agin the Government." How could Aristophanes attack the oligarchs? There was no fun to be got out of them. Hence, his violent attacks upon Cleon (at least partly) and his perpetual girding against democracy. But how far was he in earnest? Goodness only knows.

Then again he attacks the new learning: the *Clouds* is entirely devoted to a satire upon Socrates, who is taken as the type of it. With the greatest recklessness for truth, Socrates is made out to be nothing but a Sophist of the worst kind, a teacher of immoral doctrines. The scientific theories of the Ionian "nature philosophers," for which we know that he had not the slightest sympathy, are thrust upon him. The promises of the rhetorician are put into his mouth. The very sophists upon whom he waged unrelenting war are all gathered up into a bundle and labelled Socrates, and combined with the personal peculiarities which marked him out as a natural butt for comedy. Was Aristophanes in earnest? He was a personal friend of Socrates, and on very good terms with him.

Euripides represented in literature the spirit of this new learning, which ruined the simplicity and grandeur of tragedy as it ruined everything else in the old order of things. And so he comes in for a copious rain of abuse. Was Aristophanes in earnest? He was a man of taste.

In these last instances you will say that this is not a revolt against the constraint of the higher life at all. To revolt in the name of Aeschylus against Euripides is certainly not the revolt of the lower against the higher. No, but it *is* the revolt of the plain "common sense" man within us against ideas, philosophy, new notions which are difficult to grasp and comprehend unless we have been brought up in them. It is the same sort of uprising as we find among plain people against science, true or false, against new ideas in politics, right or wrong, against new schools of painting or music. And here, indeed, Molière walks hand in hand with Aristophanes. The indolent conservative within us is higher than the animal, but he is below the philosopher, below the man of ideas, as much as he is below the poet and creator.

But there is *one* thing against which a Greek will not rebel—art and the laws and limitations of art. As much waywardness and audacity as you please in the matter, but no tampering with the form. Obviously for an artist to rebel against the laws of his art is as suicidal as for a philosopher to try and overthrow the reason, and one might have hoped both to be impossible, but alas! experience shows that they are not. A better instance in the case of art cannot be wished for than is afforded by many of Browning's poems. No doubt it is a great nuisance and trouble to have to find rhymes when you are bursting with noble and profound thoughts; which of us has not felt that? Browning felt it so keenly that he ruined *A Grammarian's Funeral* by such rhymes as *fabric* and *dab brick*, just out of spite and as a protest against the bondage of his art. It is largely because of his carelessness for form that the stream of Rabelais wanders into desultory dull marshes, and gets choked in noisome shallows. The same defect makes *Tristram Shandy* unreadable as a whole. This is indeed the natural besetting sin of humourists of this kind, and we may be thankful to the extraordinary conservatism of Athens in questions of artistic form, that their comedy escaped it as easily as their tragedy. For the wildest effusions of humour were confined within formal limits as strict as those of tragedy.

It is only consistent and reasonable that this immense topsy-turvydom, this annihilation of the world we live in, and substitution of an airy dream in which our unsophisticated unmoral nature emerges naked and unashamed, it is only right that the whole vision should be logically carried out, and should end in a blaze of triumph, in the glorification of unrighteousness. In the *Birds* above all the wild schemer and dreamer Pisthetaerus, after building Cloudcuckootown in the air and reducing the gods to submission, marries Basileia the daughter of Zeus, and leaves the stage in a festal procession, burlesquing the attributes of Zeus himself. Modern critics have positively been offended by this climax; poetic justice, they conceive, demands that this audacious and impious rascal Pisthetaerus should be punished, that at least we should be given to understand that his triumph is but apparent. Poetic justice indeed! what has any kind of justice to do in a state of things where we are in revolt against every law? The dream of a world in which we can give full play to all our unregenerate instincts must be carried out at all hazards, the charming wild vision must be consummated and crowned, and die out like a glorious day in all the colours of the sunset. Time enough afterwards to wake up

and go back to our black coats and high hats; let us dream
the dream out.

> Ah Love! could you and I with Him conspire
> To grasp this sorry Scheme of Things entire,
> Would not we shatter it to bits—and then
> Re-mould it nearer to the Heart's Desire!

So the finale of the *Clouds* is the triumph of the average
unreflecting man over new ideas, just as that of the *Birds*
is the triumph of the natural desire of man to do what he
likes over the limitations of space and time and the laws
of the physical universe.

So closely are tragedy and comedy united in the ideas
which lie at their root. For it is precisely the enforcement
of these limitations which is the lesson of tragedy. Antigone
loses her life for a convention which a hero of the old comedy
would have laughed to scorn[1]. Ajax dies for a trifling
religious matter which Pisthetaerus would have ranked
with burglary, lying, and studies from the nude. Agamemnon is shown to us for a moment in the height of all
his glory, only that he may be struck down by a dreadful
doom. That we are to remember we are but men, that the
mightiest may not presume, that

> The glories of our blood and state
> Are shadows, not substantial things,

that we can by no means do as we like, these are the lessons
of tragedy. And the old comedy turns it all inside out, and
makes a world in which we can do exactly what we please
without fear and without reproach.

To say much about the characters of the plays, after
what has gone before, would be superfluous. The heroes,

---

[1] *Frogs*, 191. (Author's note.)

if heroes they can be called, are just what I have spoken of throughout, as the unregenerate natural man, absolutely selfish and unblushingly seeking to satisfy all his instincts, except the moral, which he hasn't got. For honour and reason, decorum and decency, he cares not a fig; he is simply a very clever animal, without the moral sense yet developed in him. From the intellectual point of view, he is the average common-sense man, who will not be taken in by any "bottled moonshine" of any philosopher or sophist, who has a profound disbelief in and contempt for science and everything that is at all above the run of his own ideas[1]. Herein indeed he resembles the man of the world whom we meet in the comedy of manners, the elderly hero of Terence or Molière. But to speak of the characters of Aristophanes as if they were on the same ground altogether as those of ordinary comedy, as Lessing and other critics do, is a great mistake. The aim of the old comedy was no representation of manners with mild sarcasm upon them, but a very different thing indeed, and the characters differ accordingly. There is indeed only one parallel to them with whom I am acquainted, Panurge. Caliban also, whom I suspect of being the offspring of Panurge by Sycorax, offers strong points of resemblance.

Yet even Strepsiades and his like profess a certain morality whenever it suits them so to do. They affect, perhaps they feel, the greatest indignation at certain

[1] Hence the fact that the hero of the old comedy is an old man. The generosity and openness to impressions of youth unfit young men for the post; we want a cynic who has "seen through all that nonsense," who has "humé ses formules" as the old Marquis de Mirabeau had it, who understands the meaning of the proverb "si jeunesse savait, si vieillesse pouvait!" (Author's note.)

crimes and misdemeanours; for example, Pisthetaerus rebukes the youth who comes to him wishing to be a parricide, Strepsiades objects to the "worse reason," the personified representation of rhetoric on the wrong side, on the ground that it is immoral. Yes, but the truth is that parricide and the new sophistry are both contrary to our natural instinct. There really are certain elementary laws of morality which are now as much instincts with us as eating and drinking, and the parricide seems to us below the animal itself. Such laws as those do not interfere with our "subjectivity." And as to the "worse reason," it certainly is not its immorality that makes it a legitimate butt for the old comedy; this very Strepsiades is moving heaven and earth to escape payment of his debts. But also it must be admitted that Aristophanes is not consistent; his characters will, if it suit him, alter at a moment's notice just to raise a laugh; and in this broad farce it does not signify; there is no harm if they do. Compared with ordinary morality, one may say, the characters are im-moral; as soon as they are confronted with any *new* immorality they become moral for the nonce, they at least assume the cloak of morality to defend themselves against the unfamiliar. For that is what men dislike in ethics, as in art, in medicine, in everything else—the unfamiliar.

There is one play of Aristophanes in which all this is changed—the *Plutus*. It does not belong to the old comedy at all, but to what is called the middle comedy. Plutus the god of wealth is blind, and therefore riches are unfairly distributed. The play shows how Plutus recovers his sight, and thereupon riches are divided properly—the good man gets more and the bad man gets less. What a change! This play is positively a sermon. The hero is not our old friend at all, he is virtue suffering under undeserved poverty and rewarded at the end. The dispute between poverty and wealth may remind us of the *Clouds*, but the whole air and sentiment is different. The people are ordinary people; we are approximating to the new theory of comedy, that it should be an imitation of real life. And, indeed, on *that* ground we should be justified in saying that *Plutus* is the best of all the extant plays of Aristophanes. We are called upon to sympathise with the honest Chremylus and rejoice in his good fortune, for all the world as if he were the Vicar of Wakefield.

But the new comedy has not yet found its legs. The abstract idea of Wealth personified is, as we can now see clearly, a mistake. He would have been all very well in the old comedy, but in his present surroundings he is a bore. *L'Avare* deals with a somewhat similar subject, but in how much more satisfactory a manner! How it would be spoilt if we had a blind god coming in to talk with Harpagon! The imitation of manners collapses at once in the presence of such a creature. In the wild fantastic world of the old comedy such allegories are quite in place. When we have Socrates swinging in a basket discussing how many times a flea can jump the length of its own foot, a chorus of clouds floating in airy raiment and singing lovely melodies, an old Athenian gravely trying to cheat his creditors by the most nonsensical expedients, when we have all this astounding fabric of absurdities jostling one another, we are not in the least put out by a couple of figures coming on the stage labelled Right and Wrong, and disputing against one another. Simply because here we are not concerned with the imitation of real life at all; if we were, it would be a prodigious failure. No, what *is* a failure is not the *Clouds* but *Plutus*. It is neither fish, flesh nor fowl; it has relics of the old garments still hanging about it, while it is partly dressed in the new. Then again it has not enough plot for the comedy of manners; and so it is altogether a disappointing work, as much below the *Acharnians* and the *Birds* on the one side, as it is below *Phormio* and the *Rudens*, *Tartufe* and *Le Joueur* on the other.

There is no end to what may be said further on this fascinating subject, which has here been only treated from one side, and that inadequately enough. But if you have got as far as this you are sufficiently bored, and I bethink me of another story.

Two respectable citizens, men of a dignified prosperity, were walking down Piccadilly and one of them holding forth to the other. Let him tell it in his own words, as he told it to somebody else, who told it to a friend of mine who told it to me. "I had got rather a nice point about Home Rule, and I had been explaining it with perspicacity and some degree of eloquence for about twenty minutes, and was wondering how he would answer it and what impression I had made upon him, when he looked up and said: 'What an extraordinary thing it is that two old men like Gunn and Shrewsbury[1] should go on making such a lot of runs.'"

[1] Cricketers of the day.

LA ROCHEFOUCAULD

(Literary Society, 1902)

La Rochefoucauld

IT has been truly said by a great poet that the proper study of mankind is man. That is a fact one is apt to lose sight of in colleges and places where they make CO_2. We are rather inclined to think that the comparative value of the Medicean and other MSS of Aeschylus, the phylogenetic value of the blastoderm, or the wave length of the ultra-violet rays, is the really important thing for man to interest himself in. And à propos of this I am reminded of a saying of a man who was great alike in mathematics, science, religion and literature, the immortal Pascal. "I had passed much time," he says, "in the study of the abstract sciences; but I lost my taste for them because I could share it with so few. When I began the *study of man* I saw that these abstract studies are not *proper* to him; I saw that in throwing myself into them I wandered further from my true state than the rest of the world does in ignoring them; and so I forgave men for neglecting them. But I did think that at least I should find plenty of companions in the study of man, because it is that which is his proper study. I was mistaken. There are still fewer who study man than who study geometry." Everything in Pascal is great and astonishing; and how astonishingly true is this. In vain descended from heaven the maxim "seek to know thyself"; we do not know ourselves nor one another, and we do not seek the knowledge, for the world is too much with us, and we think the average of Mr Fry[1] or the colour of a riband to be more important to us.

[1] A cricketer of the day.

But a literary society can least of all afford to neglect that study, for literature is largely, if not entirely, the expression of man's nature. And of all those literary persons who have sought to penetrate into the recesses of the mind few have thrown a more piercing light into its secret places than the accomplished and amiable Frenchman whom we have to-day taken for our subject. Amiable I say deliberately, for amiable he was above most men, however much the world may have chosen (in its rough and ready fashion) to dub him "cynic."

Francis, Prince of Marsillac, Baron of Verteuil and Duke of La Rochefoucauld, was born 15th December 1613. At the age of sixteen he served in an Italian campaign, and thenceforward his life was divided for many years between the court and the camp. As for his military exploits, I think we will leave them on one side; he never was very greatly distinguished as a soldier, and the French wars of that century are profoundly uninteresting. But his career in politics, if politics is a word to be applied to the court intrigues of that period, was much more important. The years 1630 to 1642, during which La Rochefoucauld was between sixteen and twenty-eight, are the years of the rule of Cardinal Richelieu, the greatest ruler of France between Louis XI and Napoleon. But his rule was no easy matter. By the ascendancy of his character and the force of his will he had subdued the weak and obstinate King, Louis XIII, to himself, but to keep him in leading-strings was an incessant struggle. On the other side was the Queen, Anne of Austria, more celebrated for the beauty of her hands and arms than for any more solid qualities of head and heart, eternally intriguing in a senseless sort of way with the Spaniards or anybody else whose interests were opposed to those of France, surrounded by busybodies and bad counsellors such as Mme de Chevreuse, dabbling in love affairs with Dukes of Buckingham and the like, hating the King and hated by the King, and hated above all by Richelieu, who is said to have been in love with her himself once. All the more turbulent among the great nobles of France rallied round her naturally, for they all hated the Cardinal, unable to understand his greatness, refusing to see that he was making France a great power, but quite able to see that he had an awkward habit of cutting off their heads. La Rochefoucauld's own father was compromised in the enterprise which conducted the Duke of Montmorency to the scaffold, and was accordingly exiled to Blois; the young La Rochefoucauld (whom I will call by this title proleptically to save trouble) was allowed to remain at Paris, and naturally he joined the discontented party. He seems to have felt a genuine pity for the perse-cutions to which the Queen was exposed (not altogether undeservedly) and attached himself especially to her service, acting as a channel of communication between her and Mme de Chevreuse. In course of time he naturally found his way into the Bastille, but was released after only eight days, and departed to serve in the army again.

After the death of Richelieu (4th December 1642) and of Louis XIII (14th May 1643) things got worse and worse. The new King was a child, Anne of Austria was regent, and the nobles who had intrigued against Richelieu might expect to rule the roost. But if they did, they were dis-appointed. Richelieu had bequeathed a successor to chastise them, even Mazarin, and now the minister was in league with the Queen. Indeed there is evidence that Mazarin was actually secretly married to her. Richelieu had been hated and feared, Mazarin was hated and despised. A supple Italian, ever resorting to craft and falsehood, sometimes overreaching himself by his own tortuous methods, avaricious and cowardly, he did not seem the man marked out by destiny to rule an old and haughty nation proud in arms. Yet somehow or other he always emerged victorious in the end.

The civil wars which broke out under his ministry are known as the Fronde. Of all civil wars the Fronde is perhaps the most frivolous. It has been regarded as a forerunner of the great Revolution, and it is true that the people of Paris did rise because of excessive taxation, but the people were at this time only the tools of a few ambitious and unscrupulous leaders. The Duke of Beaufort, Madame de Chevreuse, who in the kaleidoscope of politics was now against her old friend the Queen, and the beautiful and fascinating Duchess of Longueville were the principal fomenters of the revolt. As for La Rochefoucauld, he had been the lover of the former lady and was now of the latter. Thus he was drawn into the discontented party, but never was of great importance in it. But these facts are significant of the whole story. A civil war raised by women in which all the actors are fighting for their own ends, in which there are no great principles involved, in which men, like Condé himself, changed over from one side to the other for some paltry motive, and which ended by the leaders all betraying the people when they could get some sop for themselves—such a war is a weariness to the flesh. To us now there are only four of the actors in it who are alive, the

immortal names of Athos, Porthos, Aramis and d'Artagnan
—four did I say? Could I forget for a moment their
devoted followers, Planchet, Bazin, Mousqueton and
Grimaud? But everybody has read the glorious series of
their exploits as set forth by the great Dumas (it may be
as well to observe that I do not mean the chemist, but the
novelist, Alexander the great as he is fondly called by us
that are his devotees). *Twenty Years After* is a sufficient
picture and a sufficient criticism of the Fronde, and on the
whole I would advise you to be content with it. *I* shall not
attempt to characterise it further, but shall simply call
attention to its natural effect on La Rochefoucauld.

To begin with, let us quote the portrait given of him by
the Cardinal de Retz. De Retz as we all know had a way
of etching in his portraits with biting acid, and he was a
personal enemy of La Rochefoucauld, yet the impression
I have got of the latter makes me think that de Retz is
pretty right in his account of him. "There has always been
something unintelligible in La Rochefoucauld," says the
Cardinal.

He has always wished to mingle in intrigues from his
childhood....He has never shown capacity for any sort
of affair, and I do not know why, for he had qualities which
would have supplied in anybody else those in which he was
wanting. His view was not wide enough and he did not
even see clearly the whole of what was within its range:
but his good sense, which was remarkable in theory, together with the sweetness of his character, his insinuating
manners and his admirable ease in intercourse with others,
ought to have made up for his lack of penetration better
than it did. He has always been a prey to irresolution, but
I do not know to what to attribute this irresolution; it
cannot come from the fruitfulness of his imagination, which

is anything but lively. I cannot attribute it to the sterility of his judgment; for though his judgment is not keen in action, he has a sound foundation of reason. We see the effects of this irresolution, without knowing the cause. He has never been apt for war, though very much a soldier; he has never been a good courtier by his own unaided efforts, though he has always had the good will to be so. He has never been a good party-man, though engaged in party all his life. The shamefaced and timid air, which marks him in society, turned in affairs into an apologetic air; he thought he had an eternal necessity for apologising, and this, taken with his maxims, which do not always show enough faith in virtue, and his practice, which has always been to back out of affairs as impatiently as he had entered into them, causes me to conclude that he had much better have discovered his own limitations and been content to pass, as he might have done, for the most polished courtier and the most honourable man in everyday life who had appeared in his time.

Such is the character of him drawn by an enemy indeed, but one of the most piercing judges of men who have ever written. Amiable, gentle, honourable, a prey to irresolution—put such a man into the surroundings in which he passed all the time of life which has most effect in forming a man's judgment of the world, mixed up with intrigues of every kind in which he was but the cat's-paw of others more practical and more unscrupulous than himself. He had seen the hollowness of all those pretenders to virtue and patriotism who sold their professions for a title or a bag of gold, he had been betrayed and befooled by those he trusted, he must have been conscious that he was himself a failure in practical life, at least of that kind, and he came out of it all a disappointed man, with a root of bitterness in him. Small wonder that his maxims are often cynical, small wonder that he who had seen the great Condé turn traitor and the contemptible Mazarin come out at the top, did not make sufficient allowance for virtue, as de Retz has it. When one considers de Retz himself, the complaint certainly seems rather impudent, and it is also worth remarking that on one occasion La Rochefoucauld spared de Retz's life. Perhaps that was what impressed de Retz so much with his irresolution. I don't think *he* would have hesitated if the advantage had been the other way.

And as the final drop in the cup of disenchantment the Duchess of Longueville, who to put it delicately was not a bit better than she should be, threw him over for some other fellow whose name is not worth remembering. La Rochefoucauld underwent all the torments of jealousy. It has been observed that of all the weaknesses of man he seeks to justify in his maxims none but jealousy—but it must be added that it is very faintly. Then in a battle he was wounded in the head and for a time lost his sight. He had now plenty of time for reflection, and this was a turning-point in his life. After a long sojourn in darkness he recovered his sight, and settled down to live in leisure and tranquillity after that stormy youth of his. He was still only forty-two, a very good age for a man, though I say it as shouldn't.

This last period of his life extends over twenty-five years, to 17th March 1680. We have come from the age of the Fronde to the age of Louis XIV, from barricades and street fighting to drawing-rooms and the interchange of compliments, from the bickerings of an aristocracy to the lifeless splendour of the Grand Monarch. Or, to put it in a word, from *Twenty Years After* to the *Vicomte de Bragelonne*.

Of La Rochefoucauld's own life in this period there is not much to say. You will find constant references to him in the letters of that divine creature Mme de Sévigné; every afternoon he and Madame de Lafayette used to sit and talk together; he in his later years crippled by gout and often suffering horribly, she also an invalid—and no wonder, for she had given birth to the modern novel—how amazed she would have been to behold the vast progeny which has sprung from her. The man who could count Mme de Sévigné and Mme de Lafayette among his devoted friends must indeed have been himself something better than a withered cynic.

The external life of La Rochefoucauld now becomes a blank, a matter of powdered wigs and shoe polish. The age of *salons* had begun, an institution peculiarly Parisian. There assembled in the drawing-rooms of the ladies who led society everyone with pretension to *esprit*, there they discussed ethical questions with avidity. Scandal and gossip no doubt had their share, but it is the eternal glory of those Parisian ladies that they at least to a large extent rose superior to their sex, and strove to make not persons but principles their theme.

Ethics were in the air; everybody was interested in ethics of some sort or other, from the frivolities of the gentleman who distinguished twelve distinct varieties of sighs to the deep earnestness of the two greatest of La Rochefoucauld's contemporaries, Pascal and Molière. Ethics in those days were really interesting, however little you who go to lectures on them may believe it. People investigated one another and themselves and wrote what they called portraits of one another and themselves. Here are some extracts from La Rochefoucauld's portrait of himself.

The conversation of people of breeding is one of the pleasures which touch me nearest. I like it to be serious and that moral questions should form the principal part of it.

I love reading in general; that which I love most is that in which something may be found to mould the intellect and fortify the soul. Above all I find extreme satisfaction in reading with a person of intelligence; for then one reflects at every moment on that which one is reading, and from the reflexions one makes on it arises the most useful and most agreeable conversation in the world.

I love my friends; and I love them in such a way that I should never hesitate a moment to sacrifice my interests to theirs. I can lower myself for them and suffer patiently their ill humours; only I do not bestow many caresses on them, and I have not any great inquietude in their absence.

That shows all the best side of the man; here is a paragraph which is more like the average view of him:

I am not very much affected by pity, and could wish I were not so at all. However, I would do anything to comfort a person in affliction, and I believe one *ought* to do anything, even to testify much compassion for his suffering, for the miserable are so foolish that this does them the greatest good in the world. But I hold also that we should be content with testifying it, and take good care not to feel it; it is a passion which serves no purpose in a well-ordered mind, which only enfeebles the heart, and which one ought to leave to the people. For the people do nothing for reason and need passions to make them do things.

There speaks the cynic, the courtier, the aristocrat, the irresolute reflecting man who puzzled de Retz because he failed in everything. What wonder? Such an one is not a leader of men, no philosopher ever was. But we find in him that strange inconsistency which though ever strange is ever so common; it is just these men who despise the multitude, who pass hard judgments on men in general, who are sceptical concerning human virtue and the truth of friendship—it is just these men who are the most devotedly attached to their friends, perhaps who are most loved by their friends. And I think that La Rochefoucauld only spoke the truth when he said he would never hesitate between his friends' interests and his own.

The principal literary occupation of that society was the composition of Memoirs and of Maxims. La Rochefoucauld wrote both, though his *Maxims* have so overshadowed his *Memoirs* that everybody knows the one and nobody the other. Never was there such a host of Memoirs as was produced about that time. Hardly an actor in the Fronde, man or woman, maid or priest, could refrain from writing his or her version of the troubles. Nobody reads them, for how can anyone read about the Fronde, except in the pages of Dumas? Certainly I would not recommend anybody to read La Rochefoucauld's. It is true that Bayle, he who wrote the great Dictionary, positively ranked them above Julius Caesar's when they first appeared—to compare them with Caesar is too ridiculous for words. In the one case the supreme man of action of all the world, narrating in a matchless style the simple record of his achievements with not a sentence superfluous nor a sentence uninteresting, in the other a meditative dreamer trying to narrate events which he could not control nor even understand, which are not interesting in themselves, and in whose account every page is dull. It is hard to believe that the *Memoirs* are the work of the author of the *Maxims* at all.

You would have expected such a man to write history like Tacitus, and instead he writes like one of our modern historians.

There is one passage however which is interesting to all readers of the *Three Musketeers*. You all remember the famous story of the diamond ornaments in that veracious chronicle; here is the original story as given by La Rochefoucauld, whether true or not, God knows:

The Duke of Buckingham, was, as I have said, a magnificent and showy person; he took great pains over his appearance in court assemblies. The Countess of Carlisle, who had a great interest in observing him, soon perceived that he made a point of wearing certain diamond ornaments which were strange to her; she had no doubt that the Queen of France had given them to him, but to make doubly sure she took the opportunity of a private conversation with the Duke at a ball in England and cut off these ornaments, intending to send them to Cardinal Richelieu. The Duke of Buckingham discovered his loss in the evening. He guessed at once that the Countess of Carlisle had taken the diamonds and feared the effects of her jealousy, thinking her quite capable of placing them in the hands of the Cardinal in order to ruin the Queen. In this extremity, he despatched that instant an order to close all the harbours of England, and forbade anyone to leave the island on any pretext whatever until a given time. Meanwhile he had a new set of diamond ornaments made like those he had lost, and sent them to the Queen, informing her of what had happened. By thus closing the harbours he stopped the Countess, and she saw that the Duke had had all the time required to countermine her plot. Thus the Queen escaped the vengeance of her angry rival, and the Cardinal lost a certain means of convicting the Queen and making certain the suspicions of the King. For it *was* the King who had given her the ornaments, which *she* had then given to Buckingham.

That is the simple story from which sprang one of the most enchanting adventures in fiction. I confess I do not believe the historian any more than the novelist—and it is a strange thing that M. d'Artagnan is never mentioned by La Rochefoucauld. I shall extract two other passages as of some interest. In the first the bitterness overflows for once from the author's heart, and we are reminded of the prevailing tone of the *Maxims*:

In the end I met with scarcely more gratitude from Mme de Chevreuse for thus ruining myself a second time to remain her friend, than I had found in the Queen. Madame de Chevreuse forgot in her exile all that I had done for her as easily as the Queen had forgotten my services when she was able to repay them.

That is what comes of putting your faith in peers and princes and such people; it is not a school for learning belief in human virtue.

My second extract throws a light on the failure of the *Memoirs* and on the character of the actors in the Fronde.

It is almost impossible to write a really exact account of the disturbances, because those who set them going, being influenced by bad motives, have taken care to prevent their being known. They feared that posterity would accuse them of devoting the happiness of their country to their own private interests. Besides this reason, it is difficult enough for anyone recounting the affairs of his own time to keep his passions so pure that he shall not abandon himself to hate or flattery, the reefs on which truth generally makes shipwreck. For myself, I propose to give a disinterested recital of all that has passed, that I may leave to the reader entire liberty to praise or blame.

That I believe is the theory of modern historians, and perhaps that is why it is impossible to read them.

But let us come to the *great* book, the *Maxims*. The popular opinion is that La Rochefoucauld is a cynic, and there is an end of him, that his book is a collection of sayings calculated to annoy, and there is an end of it, that his philosophy consists of tracing everything in us to *amour propre*, and there is an end of that. I will not deny that there is much truth in this view.

"You may be cleverer than another man," says La Rochefoucauld himself, "but you won't be more clever than *all* the others." And Goethe, who said the last word on nearly everything, has summed up this question also (I mean the question of the value of the world's opinion) in a nutshell: "there is no doubt this public, so much honoured and despised, is almost always wrong in particulars, hardly ever in its broad views."

The broad view then, we may take it, is correct; La Rochefoucauld is a cynic, his *Maxims* do annoy, and he is fond of setting down *amour propre* as the mainspring of our actions.

We will take the three points in order. And with regard to the first, it is natural to begin with asking what we mean by calling him a cynic. Historically, the Cynics were a sect of the followers of Socrates; why they were called Cynics nobody knows, but their chief peculiarities consisted in the exaggeration of certain of the salient points in the character of Socrates. That extraordinary man was in part an ascetic; he disdained appearances, never wore shoes even in the coldest winter, was content to live on bread and water, and considered a moral life alone sufficient for happiness. These sides of his manifold character the Cynics took up and exaggerated, neglecting all the rest. Diogenes in his tub, despising Alexander the Great (not Dumas this time but the Macedonian) in the height of his glory, is the extreme type of them. According to their name, they lived like dogs, and shut themselves off from all the highest life of man, representing that revolt against civilisation which crops up every now and then in so many times and places. Such a life necessarily leads to a low view of human nature. He who is content to live like an animal must needs look on man as an animal and nothing more, however much he may prate of virtue, which he does not understand. For the virtue of man is the virtue of a social being whose reason has raised him above the animals. And the Cynics were not even social animals. And as for *their* virtue, it was purely negative, being nothing but the avoidance of all those desires which bind us to enjoyments.

In modern times the meaning of the word has changed. The cynic is no longer the Indian fakir who dwells like a solitary animal in the woods absorbed in the contemplation of himself. But he is a person who looks on man from a low standpoint, who like Diogenes despises all glory and all the varnish of civilisation, who loves to draw out the animal nature or at any rate the selfishness of man. That he speaks the truth is true, but it is not the whole truth. That he speaks the truth is indeed just what people complain of, for if he did not he would be harmless, but he speaks truths which are unpleasant. People generally do not like either what is true or what is false, so far simply as it is true or false; they like what is pleasant to them. They like being flattered because then they hear what is pleasant but false, they like hearing a pleasant truth still better because it is pleasant and true.

When thus La Rochefoucauld is called a cynic I take it that what it comes to is this, that he speaks unpleasant truths, and that he does not speak the whole truth. And if there is anything calculated to make one a cynic is it not just this, that a man who forces you to contemplate a truth you do not like should be called a cynic, that you should therefore refuse to listen to him and should think you have disposed of him and his arguments because you have labelled him with a nickname? But I think better of you who are here present, for I perceive that you are listening to me.

But he does not speak the whole truth! No, I daresay not, and should very much like to know how many writers do. But it does not occur to people to complain of some amiable writer who wears rose-coloured spectacles and sees everything through a haze of benevolence and sentimentality, a Dickens for example—it does not occur to them to complain that "he does not speak the whole truth and therefore we will not read him." What right have you to expect the whole truth? Would it not be better to consider first which sort of writer is more likely to do you good? If indeed one were compelled to confine oneself to one or other kind, I would say, "keep the benevolent gentleman with his spectacles, and leave the teller of unpleasant truths alone." But there is no such compulsion, and in fact the case is very much the other way. Everywhere we meet with the pleasant truths and the pleasant falsehoods, whether in books or in life; and it spoils us. It is a good thing to brace oneself a little with the tonic of a La Rochefoucauld now and then. It is a good thing to be reminded that the agreeable illusions of youth, the ebullient enthusiasms of friendly conversation, the protestations which are truly meant at the time, will often fail to stand the test of time, that after all other people are more concerned with themselves than with you, that as La Rochefoucauld says "gratitude is often nothing but a lively sense of favours to come." Else if we persist in thinking too well of men we may find the day when our illusions shall be stripped from off us, and we see the world as it is and it will horrify us and we shall turn misanthropical and curse mankind and die. Are not these things written for our edification in the *Phaedo* of Plato and in Shakespeare's *Timon of Athens*?

Call then La Rochefoucauld a cynic if you like, but let that only be the greater reason for taking his bitter medicine, be it only as an antidote after the manner of Mithradates King of Pontus.

Besides I cannot help thinking that this charge of cynicism is somewhat exaggerated. I remember the golden saying, one of the shortest of all, "on pardonne tant que l'on aime." I remember those two beautiful sayings which better than any others illuminate the very heart of friendship: "It is more shameful to distrust one's friends than to be deceived by them." And again: "We cannot love anything except in its relation to us, and we only follow our own taste and our own pleasure when we prefer our friends to ourselves: nevertheless by this preference alone can friendship be true and perfect."

Those are not bad epigrams for a cynic to make, and not easily will you find anything more beautiful and more true.

But it is time to be getting on to the second objection, that the *Maxims* annoy. This is precisely the proof that they are true. When Swift tells us that we are Yahoos, in

every respect inferior to his Houyhnhnms, we do not care;
we only laugh at it because we know it is not true nor
anywhere near it. But to read La Rochefoucauld is to be
put to one perpetual blush. Do not mind it; it is a good
thing and very becoming, especially if one has a fair com-
plexion; blushing has always been held to be a mark of
modesty and ingenuousness. It *is* annoying for an elderly
person like me to read that the old are fond of giving good
advice because they are no longer able to give bad examples.
Or that we think we are leaving our vices when it is our
vices that are leaving us. Or that the passions of youth are
hardly more opposed to salvation than the lukewarmness
of the old. Or that we come fresh to each distinct age of
life and are apt to show a sad lack of experience in each
despite the number of our years. But *you* shall not get
off either. "Most young people think they are natural
when they are only unpolished and rude." Women especially do not love him, for much the same reason that
Byron asserts they did not like Don Juan, because he
strips off the sentiment from love and laughs at that and
everything else. I never yet met a woman who had read
La Rochefoucauld or who could abide him. They do not
like to hear that the intellect of most women serves rather
to fortify their folly than their reason. Nor that there are
few women whose merit outlasts their looks. Nor that it
is with true love as with ghosts: everybody talks of it and
nobody has seen it.

But I confess that it seems to me that when La Rochefoucauld talks of women he does not hit the mark as he
does with men. He talks from the average male standpoint,
which is absurd. And yet he spent all his life under the

influence of women. Besides his early love affairs, in his sober autumn he was the devoted friend of Mme de Lafayette and Mme de Sablé. And then he talks of them like that! No, the reason women don't like him is not because of what he says of *them* in particular; it is because of those maxims which apply to men and women alike, and which are not absurd at all, unfortunately. Such as "whatever good we hear of ourselves, we never hear anything new to us." And "there is no man who believes himself inferior in *all* his qualities to that man of the world whom he thinks the most of." Yes, we all think *we* should have had the sense to clear out of Moscow before the cold weather began.

Then again there are some elderly gentlemen of my acquaintance who must feel uneasy when they read this question: "Why must we needs have memory enough to retain in its minutest details all that has happened to us, and *not* enough to remember how often we have related them to the same person?" And: "We can forgive those who bore us, but not those who are bored by us." And: "Gravity is a mystery of the body invented to hide the emptiness of the mind." I am reminded of—but never mind. And above all there is one question which made me wriggle like a worm the first time I read it: "Why is it that we all complain of our memory and none of us of our judgment?" Since then I have taken to giving myself airs on the strength of my memory and to professing that my judgment is no better than other people's. And yet here I am pronouncing confidently on La Rochefoucauld and there you all sit judging him and me and not having the slightest doubt that you are quite right.

Now for the third objection, which is thus stated by Voltaire: "There is hardly more than one truth in the book, that *amour propre* is the motive of everything." It is true, adds Voltaire, that this idea is presented under such varied aspects that it is almost always piquant. But certainly, though many of the maxims I have already quoted do *not* illustrate this theory, yet it is true that that is the prevailing idea, that is the great impression we carry away from the book.

I confess that it is difficult to come to any very clear conclusion about this matter. It seems certain that if we interpret the theory of *amour propre* to mean that we must seek our own happiness in all we do, which indeed is the foundation of utilitarianism, it is impossible to escape from admitting that it is true. The martyr prefers the flame to recantation because he would be unhappier if he recanted than he is when he burns. The man who reads papers to literary societies must, I suppose, think it would be worse still for him if he backed out of it. In whatever choice we make between alternative actions we must needs choose that which appeals the more strongly to us ourselves. We may say we sacrifice ourselves to our party, our family, or even our college. But if any man plays cricket for his college rather than for his county, it is after all because his college appeals more to him personally. There *is* no escape; we can only love things or people in their relation to us, we can only act because this or that action appeals to us. The very attempts his critics make to escape prove only that there is no escape. M. Rébelliaud, for instance, says that there are other motives for our actions, such as custom, imitation, inconsistency. And how does that help him? You *may* do a thing from custom, very true. But why do you want to keep up the custom? Because you feel it is easier for you to keep it up than to break it, because your self-love is interested in keeping it up. How many things we do through custom simply because our vanity is pleased by having a custom! Inconsistency is just the same turned inside out. And imitation; if you do a thing through imitation it is because it pleases you to imitate. Really, if M. Rébelliaud cannot find a better defence than that, he had better capitulate at once. The very reason why he and others protest against La Rochefoucauld is because to admit the truth of what he says hurts their self-love and their vanity. Their very protestations are signs that he speaks the truth. Lord Byron with all his faults was sincere and straightforward, and this is how he bursts out (*Journal*, 1st December 1813): "Curse on Rochefoucauld for being always right! In him a lie were virtue—or at least a comfort to his readers." And as Saintsbury observes, it is a great deal easier to abuse than to refute him.

But then if that is all La Rochefoucauld means, that we must be moved to everything by ourselves, it seems a truism, and nothing for respectable librarians of the Institute to get angry about.

Yet there must be something in the objections made; so much smoke would never rise without some fire beneath it. And I think the real difficulty all comes of lack of definition, as usual.

Amour propre may and does mean self-love in the sense already given to it, but of self-love there are divers kinds. It will be sufficient for the present purpose to divide it into two by the method called by Platonists dichotomy. To put it briefly, there is a good self-love and a bad self-love. When your self-love leads you to sacrifice yourself because you feel you cannot endure not to do so, that is a good self-love, which is to say that it is praised by other people. Such is the self-love of the martyr, the patriot, the man who plays cricket for his college. But the other, the bad self-love, is unfortunately much commoner; in fact it is in plain English selfishness, and in La Rochefoucauld more particularly that variety of selfishness which is called vanity. After writing all this I find it all crystallised in one of the maxims of Vauvenargues: "If there are two kinds of self-love," says he, "one which makes us hard and selfish and cruel and one which makes us compassionate and obliging to others, is that any reason for confounding the two?" By these few words Vauvenargues blows the whole edifice of La Rochefoucauld to smithereens. I often wonder that Vauvenargues is so little known in England. I fear the reason is that he takes a steady view of life as a whole and is not bitter and one-sided. Do you remember what Samuel Rogers said? He was famous for his sarcastic and malicious sayings (which indeed were much better than his poetry) and in defence of this habit of his he once said to somebody: "You see, my voice is very weak, and if I did not say ill-natured things nobody would hear me." So it is that people open their ears to La Rochefoucauld and close them like a deaf adder to Vauvenargues.

The way, then, in which I conceive that the attack upon La Rochefoucauld ought to be directed is this. It is quite true that we must be guided by self-love in all we do, even when we sacrifice self, but La Rochefoucauld lays too much stress, lays we may say the *whole* stress of his criticism of man upon the inferior kind of self-love, upon selfishness and vanity. The better kind does appear in him once or twice, but not often. Especially in that noble maxim concerning friendship, which I have quoted once and will quote again, for never can one repeat it too often. "We cannot love anything except in its relation to us, and we only follow our own taste and our own pleasure when we prefer our friends to ourselves: nevertheless by this pre-ference alone can friendship be true and perfect." Therein lies already the whole of the distinction I have just striven to elaborate a little. Therein shine out the human eyes for once from behind the mask in which he chose to shroud himself.

Was he conscious himself or not of what he was doing? Did he deliberately confound the two meanings of self-love? I think not; I think he got into the way of seeking after the motives of men, and saw that all must needs come of self-love in some sense, and was misled into too low a view of man's nature in consequence, partly by the ruinous education he had gone through, partly by an ambiguity and the *generally* bad meaning of the term *amour propre*, partly by the mere fact that grubbing after motives necessarily leads men to take such a view.

In this connexion I remember an interesting story which Mme de Rémusat tells of Napoleon. Never, she says, did any man carry the habit of seeking for motives in men to such a pitch as he. Shortly before his Egyptian expedition, he went to visit Talleyrand who was lying ill. He talked with such enthusiasm of his plans that he quite carried away the cautious and hard and selfish diplomat, who in a moment of generosity said: "There is a large sum of money lying in that drawer, take it if it will help you and I will chance your repaying it." Napoleon took it, went to Egypt, lost his army, came back, became First Consul, and repaid the money. But he said when he repaid it: "I have been puzzling ever since you lent me this money to find out what conceivable motive you can have had for doing it, and I cannot imagine what it can have been." Talleyrand answered that there wasn't any, that it was in an access of generous enthusiasm. "Then," said Napoleon, "you were a dupe."

That is what comes of carrying to an extreme the habit of seeking after motives. And this brings me to another way of putting it. One may divide self-love into conscious and unconscious; the unconscious lies at the root of all that we praise and call virtue, the conscious we blame. And La Rochefoucauld's mistake may be said to come of representing all our actions as coming from conscious self-love and neglecting the unconscious. That is what it comes to when de Retz complains that he does not allow enough to virtue. And that of course is the natural pit for a man to fall into who thinks about these things. He who thinks about motives must be conscious of them, and will easily give too much weight to conscious springs of action. But that sort of self-love which produces what we call unselfishness is unconscious, and here it is that La Rochefoucauld's analysis fails. Most men are not conscious of their motives, because, as Pascal found, there are even fewer men interested in the study of man than in the study of geometry.

Moreover unluckily, for this same reason, a great deal of the worse self-love is also unconscious. We do not know how vain we are. Pascal himself lays as much stress on this as ever did any cynic. "Those who write against glory," he says, "wish to have the glory of having written well, and those who read wish to have the glory of having read it; and I myself who write this have perhaps this desire, and perhaps those who read it will have it too." It is in this unveiling of the unconscious vanity and selfishness of the mind that the true and terrible force of La Rochefoucauld lies. No other ever laid bare with such sagacity all those secret nerves, which ache under his scalpel. "That which renders the pain of shame and of jealousy so keen, is that vanity cannot be called in to support them." "What makes the vanity of others intolerable, is the fact that it wounds our own." "What we call liberality is most often only the vanity of giving, which we love better than what we give." "We easily forget our faults when they are only known to ourselves." How horribly true and undeniable all these things are, and yet to which of us do they not come like flashes of light to reveal our own deformity? That is why Byron cursed La Rochefoucauld in his vehement way, why so many will not endure him and why some are drawn to him by a dreadful fascination.

Yes, it is indeed quite true that this is the principal impression which we get from the maxims, as the innumerable facets on the eye of an insect unite in an impression on the insect's brain. The more astonishing is it that he has contrived to present this idea in so many forms and with such perpetual freshness. Every time it seems to be new. But then it is interspersed with many other

ideas which do not come under the same head at all. For
of order and arrangement in the book there seems to be
none. Here and there you get little groups of maxims
which are connected, but generally speaking they seem
thrown together at random. But if there is no particular
form about the book as a whole, the form of each separate
maxim is perfection, and a deal of polishing it took to
bring them to it, as you may see by comparing the earlier
versions with the final.

But it is not a book to be continually with one after all.
The squirrel gyrates wonderfully in his cage, but it is a cage,
and now and then a breath from the outside world comes
upon one and one longs to escape from cages and drawing-
rooms. After reading twenty or thirty of these perfect
epigrams, what a change it is to recall some of those great
sayings of the truly inspired men who never were corrupted
as La Rochefoucauld was by evil communications. Think of
that hard saying of Spinoza, which indeed should be
treasured up and fed upon in our hearts, "He who truly
loves God must not expect to be loved in return," or that
which Goethe drew from it, as he confesses, "If I love thee,
what is that to thee?" Or take that question so beautifully
treated by Aristotle, Why is it that he who confers benefits
loves more than he who receives them? La Rochefoucauld
would have said (I do not know that he actually does) that
the recipient loves less because his vanity or self-love is
hurt by being in an inferior position, whereas the self-love
of him who confers the benefit is flattered. And much truth
there may be in that, but how much more noble is Aristotle's answer. He who confers the benefit stands to him
who receives in some sort as the artist to his own work or

the parent to his own child, and therefore loves the more of the two, just as the poet loves exceedingly his own poems, rejoicing in them as if they were his children. More noble and beautiful is that and surely not less true in the case of all those unsophisticated and uncorrupted who have kept themselves unspotted from the world. And it is better on the whole to cling to those nobler views; little enough we may all be, and good it may be to realise that now and then, but if we cannot be good for very much, let us at least like children play at being good, for it is of such, and not of La Rochefoucauld, that is the kingdom of heaven.

LUCIAN

(Literary Society, 1905)

Lucian

IT is written in the *Life of Lord Macaulay* that he was as
well acquainted with his Lucian as most literary men are
with Voltaire. The statement is made with uplifted eye-
brows, an air of surprise. It wakes in turn surprise in the
mind of the classical scholar. It is very remarkable, he
thinks to himself, that the chosen youth of England, all
the boys in all the schools who are not too stupid to do
anything but Science and Modern Languages, should spend
many years in the acquisition of the Classics and should
make so little use of them, when they have got them, that
they positively know their Voltaire and do not know their
Lucian. They pick up a little French in an odd hour or two
under the supervision of an amiable and incompetent
Frenchman who has been a failure in his own country.
They spend many hours every week in studying the
Classics under the guidance of men who have distinguished
themselves at the Universities in cricket, football and
athletic sports. And the end of it is that they do not know
their Lucian and probably imagine that he was a Latin
poet put to death by Nero for writing one of the most
tedious epics upon record.

After spending much valuable time in considering this
problem, I believe I have at length arrived at a satisfactory
solution. The classical student becomes so highly trained
in the pure idioms of Attic Greek that he is shocked by the
occasional lapses from it in the pages of this delightful
Syrian. It is true—it must be admitted with regret—that
Lucian *is* shaky in his uses of μή and οὐ. Yet I beseech you

not to be too much influenced by this. The correct use of μή and οὐ is after all not absolutely everything in literature. There are excellent authors who do not attempt to write Attic Greek at all, there are authors of repute who do not even know any—for example Mr George Moore and St Paul. Lay aside for once this literary purism, and condescend to take a glance at a man who is much more amusing and delightful reading than most of the people you toil through in pursuit of a degree.

Lucian was born somewhere about A.D. 120 at a place called Samosata, in Syria, on the banks of the Euphrates. Of his early years little enough is known. His parents thought a liberal education too expensive, so he was sent to a school of art, poor boy. His uncle was a sculptor of some sort, and the nephew was taken into his shop. One day was enough for Lucian, he broke a slab of marble, his uncle thrashed him, he came home in tears and, of course, his mother took his part. That night, if we may believe Lucian's own account (though it is generally better *not* to believe what he says) he dreamed a dream. Two women, whom in modern language we may interpret as the genius of the Slade and the genius of the Faculty of arts, laid hold of him and struggled for him so that he was nearly rent in twain; Lucian chose wisely, deserted the Slade for ever and went in for arts. In those days that meant that he became a rhetorician. He wandered about the world from Syria to Gaul lecturing on rhetoric and the art of public speaking. Somewhere about 160 he gave up rhetoric also, because he judged it to be little better than flat lying (and men were not made prime ministers in those days for their skill in "lying in state at Westminster," as a late acquaintance of ours did both before and after death). So he went and settled at Athens, where he perfected that beautiful Attic style which is so remarkable in a man brought up on the banks of the Euphrates. For though he never did get some little details right, which are now taught to mere beginners, he yet wrote a Platonic Greek which on the whole is most beautiful and admirable. Late in life he was appointed to some sort of Government office, but it was a sinecure and only intended to keep him comfortable in worldly goods, probably the War Office. Much plagued with gout in his age (a subject on which he wrote an amusing mock tragedy) he finally died, it is said a hundred years old.

The time at which he lived was very interesting. The old order was changing, yielding place to new, nor was it yet clear in which particular way the change would come in the thought of men. The beautiful and withal absurd old Paganism, the religion of Artemis crowned with the crescent moon hunting in the woodlands, of golden Aphrodite rising from the salt sea, of Zeus shaking Olympus with his nod and kicking his son out of heaven and beating his wife, of Dionysus reeling ripe among a rout of Silenuses and Bacchantes—all this had long become incredible and ridiculous. It is true that in the lifetime of Lucian a desperate attempt was made to make the dry bones live, as yet later it was to be again under Julian. But it was a galvanic business at the best. And as those venerable oak trees gradually mouldered into dust, there sprang up about them a whole wilderness of new and fantastic growths, men believed everything and nothing, Apollonius of Tyana worked miracles and founded a sort of sect, that incredible impostor Alexander of Abonutichus did the like, a monstrous rout of Oriental religions invaded the vacant ground, the dog-headed Anubis, Isis with her sistrum and Mithra with his bull—in Tiberim defluxit Orontes—all the ghosts came out in the twilight after their fashion, even as we now see in the decay of faith people, presumably sane, resorting to palmistry and table-turning, dwelling uncomfortably for a week together in haunted houses to study spiritual manifestations, and speculating seriously on the question whether hobgoblins do or do not wear clothes. Among the other innumerable sects was one called Christians, generally supposed to be exceedingly mischievous, to be principally occupied with the worship of an ass's head and to be a mere variety of Judaism on just the same footing as the rest. It was by no means yet clear that Christianity would beat the rest—those learned in such matters declare positively that about the end of the second century it seemed to be a turn of the scale whether Christ or Mithra should prevail—Mithra was worshipped by countless thousands throughout the Empire; for instance, along the line of the Roman occupation in the north of Britain the legionaries have left innumerable relics of his cult. To Lucian all of these things were on the same footing, and he laughed at all with equal impartiality and equal wit. Perhaps the best specimen of his attacks upon the established religion is the dialogue called—let us say Jupiter-Irving. Jupiter is shown in a great state of mind, ranting in high-flown iambic verses:

O man's first disobedience and the fire
That wretch Prometheus stole from heavenly hearths!
To be a god or not—that is the question—
Ye quivers with three-bolted thunder stored—
With ever burning sulphur unconsumed—

Athena entreats him to condescend to explain—"*we* haven't swallowed Euripides wholesale," she says, "and can't keep it up in that strain." Juno says sarcastically *she* knows what's the matter—it's some new love affair of Jupiter's, but he says it's much more serious—it's just a toss-up whether the gods are to be honoured any longer. Two philosophers—let us say Professor Huxley and the Archbishop of Canterbury—have been disputing about Providence in the nineteenth century—Huxley says there are no gods and that the world is a matter of chance and natural selection—the excellent Archbishop did his best to keep his end up—but they agreed to put it off till to-day. "So," says Jupiter, "you see what a fix *we're* in." They decide to hold an assembly of all the gods—proclamation is made and the gods assemble, but there is a great dispute about precedence—some of them are made of gold, and unluckily the golden gods are generally outlandish heathen deities, the best are mostly only marble or bronze, or per- haps a hollow shell of ivory and gold but wooden inside, honeycombed by whole colonies of mice and rats. Jupiter has decided they shall sit in order according to their value, and Neptune is very wrath that a dog-faced Egyptian god should sit above *him*. However they get settled at last, amid great tumult, the more vulgar gods crying out— "Divide, divide the sacrifices! This is thirsty work, where's the nectar and ambrosia? One god, one victim." Jupiter gets on his legs to make a speech, but is very nervous— Mercury suggests he should begin with Demosthenes, so he starts with a Philippic, slightly altered for the occasion: "I believe you would give a great deal, men of—er— Heaven, to know why it is that you are here assembled, and therefore I beg of you to give me your best attention. It is impossible to exaggerate the importance of the present crisis, and yet *we* appear to pay no attention to it. I wish now (for truth is Demosthenes is running dry) just to tell you what is the matter." And so he explains. None of the other gods have any advice to offer, but Mephistopheles gets up and has the face to tell the gods it's all their own fault—their oracles are so deplorably ambiguous—they don't do anything but sit and gobble up sacrifices. This sets some of the others on their defence, but they only make themselves ridiculous. Meantime the controversy between the two philosophers begins again upon earth, and the gods lean downward and listen. The Archbishop brings his artillery to bear on the profane Huxley, but is ignominiously defeated at every point, until the dignitary of the Church fairly loses his temper, calls the other all the bad names he can lay his tongue to, accuses him of having murdered his brother, of corrupting the youth like Socrates, and of making speeches in the Union in defence of the Boers. So ends the discussion, and the only consolation for the gods is that all the rabble in Greece believes in them after all, and *all* the savages without exception. "Ah," says Jupiter sadly, "that is all very well, but you know what Darius says in Herodotus, about Zopyrus who won Babylon for him—I'd rather have one man like that on my side than a million Babylons."

The more intellectual classes were the prey of philosophy. Centuries before this Alexander the Great had murdered his intimate friend Clitus in one of those fits of drunken fury to which that great and amiable prince was given. He shut himself up (being sober) in an agony of remorse and shame—what did his attendants do?—they solemnly sent in two philosophers to comfort him. I imagine to myself an unfortunate student who in an unguarded moment has written down the statement that the vagus nerve connects with the Fallopian tubes and has been consequently ploughed—I imagine him sitting with his head in his hands and his whisky untasted beside him—I like to dwell on the picture of the maid servant announcing two gentlemen to speak with him and (in spite of his protesting a desire for solitude) ushering in—Professor Read and Mr Grieve. Yes, in those days philosophy was a serious matter, and conceived that she had a work to do in the world. And while Lucian was sharpening his jests in Athens the man on whom rested the whole weight of the civilised world was no other than the great and wise and good and sad Emperor Marcus Aurelius Antoninus, he round whose head rests the last halo of the ancient world, fulfiller of the dream of Plato, the philosopher made king. Like King Arthur he fought in the mist the last battle of the old against the new, and when he died the brand Excalibur was cast away. So lofty, so severe are his *Meditations* that they pierce us like the cold stars of winter; everything human is purged out of him. This was the last word of the wisdom of Greece:

Either gods or atoms. Either confusion and entanglement and scattering again, or unity, order, providence. If the first, why do *I* wish to live amid the clashings of chance and chaos? or care for aught else but to become earth myself at last? and why am I disturbed, since this dispersion (death) will come whatever I do? But if the latter case be true, I reverence and stand firm and trust in him who rules.

Thus wags the world up and down from age to age. And either the universal mind determines each event; and if so, accept thou that which it determines. Or it has ordered once for all and all follows in sequence. Or invisible elements are the origin of all things. In a word, if there be a god, then all is well; if all things go at random, act not at random thou.

It is pure Agnosticism—for that also is no new thing in the world—but in that faith lived and died the highest recorded type of pure duty. It is good to go and look on his marble bust in the British Museum; it is not beautiful, but in gazing on it one feels there are better things in the world than beauty, and hears him saying in the last words of the *Meditations*: "Depart thou then contented, for he that releaseth thee is content."

Against philosophy in such a form what man should dare to breathe a word? Well, *some* people do—and their word is prig. But the world was full of philosophers of very different kinds. Quarrelsome were they, vain as peacocks, preaching one thing and doing another, wearing long beards and ragged cloaks and talking organised nonsense. Upon these Lucian fell with joy. He so bantered and badgered them that they got seriously angry (or else he pretends so) and he condescended to defend himself by saying that he only attacked impostors and not the real thing—just as Molière said, though with both Molière and Lucian it is difficult to distinguish. And indeed the man whose trade is to laugh has a way of laughing at what he respects as much as what he doesn't.

In one of his most celebrated dialogues Mercury is represented as holding an auction and putting up the philosophers for sale. He begins with Pythagoras. "Gentlemen," says the auctioneer, "we here offer you a philosopher of the very best and most select description—who buys? who wants to be a cut above the rest of the world? Who wants to understand the harmonies of the universe, and the transmigration of souls? Who would like to be a vegetarian and live a second life in the form of a peacock?" Pythagoras fetches a high price, being knocked down to a syndicate of philosophers from Asia Minor for £40. Diogenes the Cynic goes for three halfpence, and Mercury gladly jumps at even that offer. Socrates fetches £8, Aristotle no less than £80. Last comes the sceptic Pyrrho, what we nowadays call a neo-Berkeleyan, a sect which now flourishes at a place sufficiently described if I say that it is generally rather behind the times and in particular behind Cambridge. A customer asks him a few questions.

Customer. Tell me, now, what do you know?
Pyrrho. Nothing.
C. What do you mean?
P. That nothing seems to me certain.
C. Are we ourselves nothing?
P. Well, that is what I am not sure of.
C. Don't you know whether you are anything yourself?
P. That is what I am still more in doubt about.
C. What a creature of doubts it is! And what are those scales for, pray?
P. I weigh arguments in them, and balance them one against another; and then, when I find them precisely equal and of the same weight, why, I find it impossible to tell which of them is true.
C. Well, is there anything you can do in any other line of business?
P. Anything, except catch a runaway slave.
C. And why can't you do that?
P. Because, you see, I've no faculty of *apprehension*.

C. So I should think—you seem to me quite slow and stupid. And now, what do you consider the main end of knowledge?

P. Ignorance—to hear nothing and see nothing.

C. You confess yourself blind and deaf then?

P. Yea, and void of sense and perception, and in no wise differing from a worm.

C. I must buy you. (*To Mercury*) What shall we say for him?

Mercury. An Attic mina.

C. Here 'tis. Now, fellow, have I bought you or not—tell me?

P. Well, it's a doubtful question.

C. Not at all—at least I've paid for you.

P. I reserve my opinion on that point; it requires consideration.

C. Follow me, at all events—that's a servant's duty.

P. Are you sure you're stating a fact?

C. There's the auctioneer, and there's the money, and there are the bystanders to witness.

P. Are you sure there are any bystanders?

C. I'll have you off to the grinding-house, sir, and make you feel I'm your master by very tangible proofs.

P. Stay—I should like to argue that point a little.

The sequel to this dialogue is called *The Resuscitated Philosophers.* It begins with Lucian flying for his life, pursued by a multitude of wrathful philosophers who have got permission to come up from the world of the dead to punish him. They are led by Socrates, crying: "Pelt the wretch, heave half a brick at him—oyster shells—anything. Hit him in the eye, Plato, and you Chrysippus, and you! He is the common enemy of all. What, tired already, Epicurus? You luxurious idle dog! Be men, philosophers, summon all your pluck; Aristotle, do run a little faster. —Good, we've caught the beast." Then they propose different punishments, but Lucian demands a fair trial. Diogenes (angry above the rest at having been sold for such a trifle at the auction) acts as accuser. Of course, Lucian is triumphantly acquitted.

The *Death of Peregrinus* is one of the works most interesting to us, because it is in that that we hear most of the Christians. This Peregrinus had been a bad lot in his youth, had then become a Christian and held high office in the Church (I have known cases of the kind myself) but got into trouble again, was expelled from the Church, expelled from Rome by the authorities, tried to make the people of Elis revolt against the Empire, an enterprise about as hopeful as the Jameson raid, and at last finding his influence waning among them, gave out that he would solemnly burn himself like Hercules at the next Olympic festival. And he actually did—Lucian was present and thus describes it.

The more foolish of the crowd shouted "Live, for the sake of the Greeks!" But the more hard-hearted cried "Fulfil your promise!" At this the old man was not a little put out, for he had expected that they would surely all lay hold on him, and not let him get into the fire, but force him to live against his will. But this exhortation to keep his promise fell on him quite unexpectedly, and made him paler than ever, though his colour looked like death before. He trembled, and became silent....When the moon rose (for she too must needs look upon this grand sight) he came forward, clad in his usual dress, and followed by his train of Cynics, and specially the notorious Theagenes of Patrae, well fitted to play second in such a performance. Peregrinus too carried a torch; and approaching the pile—a very large one, made up of pitch-pine and brushwood—they lighted it at either end. Then the hero (mark what I say) laid down his scrip and his cloak, and stood in his under-garment—and very dirty it was. He next asked for frankincense to cast on the fire; and when some one brought it, he threw it on, and turning his face towards the south (this turning towards the south is an important point in the performance) he exclaimed "Shades of my father and my mother, be propitious, and receive me!" When he had said this, he leaped into the burning pile and was seen no more, the flames rising high and enveloping him at once.

It is evident that the Christians could not well blame Lucian for his account of this impostor, who had made a good thing out of it by swindling the Christians themselves. And Lucian's account of Christianity itself is really a very fair one and remarkably accurate. It is true it calls it an "extraordinary philosophy," and says with compassion "these poor wretches persuade themselves that they shall be immortal and live for ever, so that they despise death and some of them offer themselves to it voluntarily." But on the whole he speaks of them with respect, and his attitude is much that of an ordinary educated Englishman, twenty years ago, towards the Salvation Army. Very different was the general public opinion of those days.

However, in later times Christian writers were as angry with him as ever the philosophers had been. They invented a story that he died by being torn to pieces by dogs. Suidas amiably observes: "Wherefore he paid a sufficient penalty for his madness in the present life, and in the future he shall inherit eternal fire together with Satan." Suidas, the horrid dull dog! I remember what a wise man once said—"If you want climate go to Heaven, if you want society—."

The third great subject for the licensed jester is politics—indeed it properly should come first. Unfortunately the

jester very often finds this field occupied with a large board
and written upon it "Trespassers will be prosecuted. By
Order." Neither Plautus nor Rabelais nor Cervantes nor
Molière nor Voltaire could open their mouths upon this
subject—they would have had the police down upon them
and have been prosecuted for *lèse-majesté* at once. If any
German happens to be present, I should like to explain
that I am making no allusion to the great Kaiser. So great
is the advantage of living under free institutions. Political
satire was the life blood of the old Attic Comedy, it was
one of the most formidable weapons in the arsenal of Swift
and Byron. As for the unlucky Lucian, there were simply
no politics to talk about. In Rome he might have been
stopped by the police, in Athens or Samosata or Gaul he
had no chance of arousing their suspicions. The great
Roman Empire lay with a dead weight upon everything.
He grew up under the rule of Hadrian, that admirable
Emperor who spent his time touring about the Empire
like the Viceroy of India and seeing that the machinery
worked right everywhere. From 138 to 183, the period of
his manhood, the two Antonines held the sceptre. The age
of the Antonines is looked upon as a sort of golden age of
happiness and tranquillity—happy the people may be that
have no history, but the political satirist is not happy. The
machinery worked right enough—men reaped the fields
and women did the washing and talked about their work
and deplored the weather, and the taxes were gathered in
regularly and everything was managed for the best—it
might have suited Pangloss, but everything was dead and
dull. Now and then there might be a diversion somewhere:
in the year 135 the Romans killed 580,000 Jews in Judea,

in the reign of Aurelius there was a terrible plague and the barbarians began invading on the north-east frontier; but of political life there was none and I do not believe there is a single political allusion in all Lucian's works. One only has to think of the *Acharnians, Gulliver*, the *Vision of Judgement*, to feel what a loss this is to the satirist. In his last years the throne of Aurelius, by the irony of fate, was occupied by that brutal gladiator Commodus, as though Caliban were the son and successor of Prospero: it is all the same to Lucian—it was all the same to the vast machinery of the Empire.

But Sophocles well said that man can devise a remedy for all things but death. When literature has utterly run to seed, man writes novels. What we call novels now had not yet been evolved, but stories of a sort were beginning to be written. Lucian wrote a remarkable story called *The Dream* or *The Cock*, of which for several reasons I shall say nothing: a more celebrated work, which may be called if not a novel at least a romance, is the *True History*.

The *True History* is perhaps the most famous work of Lucian, certainly that which has had the greatest influence upon later literature. It itself derives from a no less venerable work than the *Odyssey*, as Lucian very fairly owns in his preface. Of all travellers' tales which have ever bewitched mankind the most enchanting are those which Odysseus told to the Phaeacians, concerning the Cyclops with his one eye, and Circe and the pigs, and the cannibal giants, and the bag of the winds, and his descent to Hades. Lucian says in his bantering way that Odysseus fired off all this stuff at the Phaeacians because he found them to be good simple easy-going folk who would swallow anything he chose to give them: Odysseus according to him was a de Rougemont and Alcinous was qualified by his innocence to be president of the British Association. Then there were other writers calling themselves historians who told enormous falsehoods, at all of whom Lucian is gibing. "We set sail once upon a time," he says vaguely, "from the Straits of Gibraltar." After some ten days during which their adventures are nothing very notable, they were seized by a whirlwind and carried up into the air some 850 miles—then they drove before the wind till they came to the Moon, where, being seized upon by the Vulture Guards, cavalry riding upon three-headed vultures as big as ships, they were brought before the king, no other than Endymion, who appears for a wonder not to have been asleep. Endymion was about to go out to battle against Phaethon, king of the Sun, and invited them to join as military attachés. The most remarkable of his troops were the flea-archers, who rode upon fleas each as big as twelve elephants. There is a pretty touch at the end of the catalogue of troops. "We heard that 70,000 Ostrich-acorns (whatever they may be) were expected from the stars beyond Cappadocia, and 5000 Horse-cranes, but I did not see them for they never came. So I thought it better not to describe their character, for what we were told of them was marvellous and quite incredible." The infantry fought upon a woven floor wrought by spiders, for the spiders there are about as big as the Isle of Wight. It really does not matter which side won, one cares no more about that than about the College Office. It is more interesting to investigate the customs of the inhabitants of the Moon and in particular their drink, which was "air squeezed into a cup yielding a liquid like dew." We classical scholars are amused every now and then by the scientific people proclaiming as a new discovery something which was quite familiar to the ancients—you see that liquid air is a regular chestnut—and then Olszewsky and Dewar dispute about who discovered it! We could tell them a good many things if we thought it worth while to condescend so far.

How they came down again into the Ocean, how a whale of 200 miles long swallowed them, how they found inside the whale an island with trees and cabbages, and cormorants and kittiwakes roosting in the branches (rather odd natural history, but perhaps birds who live in whales have to change their habits), how they went on an exploring expedition through the wood and found a temple of Neptune and an old man who had lived there for many years, how the imagination of Lucian gets heated with driving and he proceeds to describe whole kindreds and nations and tongues that dwelt about the mouth of the whale, Turbotfeet and Lobstersons, and Thunnyheads and Crabhands—how they planted vines and made wine, and so lived one year and eight months in the whale, along with many other things rather hard to believe, had best be read in Lucian. At last they got tired of it, so they set fire to the woods, beginning towards the tail, and the woods blazed with a great conflagration. "For seven days and nights the whale did not find out that anything was wrong, but on the eighth and ninth we thought he seemed a bit sick—at least he yawned more lazily than he used and shut his mouth up sooner than before. Last of all the whale died also and we got out. Then we came after a time to the island of the Blessed, which is the most charming place I

ever saw—meadows full of all manner of flowers, violet,
amaracus and asphodel—but scenery is the last refuge
of the destitute—enough to say that all good Professors
go there when they die. There I saw Socrates cross-
examining Nestor and Palamedes, and round about him
a crowd of beautiful youths—but Rhadamanthus, who
rules there, was rather annoyed with him and threatened
to turn him out if he would still be talking nonsense and
would not drop his Socratic irony and revel with the rest.
Plato was not there, because he was gone to live in his own
Republic under his own laws with Dr Jowett and Dr
Jackson—by advices last received none of the three were
on speaking terms. There also I saw the Earl of Beacons-
field with a gold crown on his head, clothed in purple and
green and orange (as he loved to be in his youth in this
world), drinking Tokay wine out of great goblets with the
three beautiful Miss Gunnings and General Gordon, who
admitted that he had been quite wrong in his ideas about
the geographical situation of Paradise. And Lord Beacons-
field told me that it was a very odd thing, but however
much wine he drank he never became Dizzy, but I did not
understand what he meant. So great are the delights of
that Paradise. And there sat Cobet and Madvig making
emendations, and they said..., and a Quain Professor of
English editing *Beowulf*, very proud because he had recovered 2571 lines unknown before, but the others said he
ought to have gone somewhere else, if *that* was to be his
way of amusing himself.

"There I might have stayed to this day in great joy and
bliss, and there is no Literary Society there, but unluckily
Helen took the opportunity of running away from Menelaus

again with one of our crew, and the end of it was we were all turned out.

"One of the next places we came to was the Island of the Damned, over which Abdul the Sultan is king. This is a very unpleasant place, full of kings and prime ministers and bad poets and Deans and Mr Stead. Then I saw that Dante was right when he put the traitors in the lowest place of all, for in the worst pit were Judas and Ephialtes the Malian and Vellidos Dolfos and Mordred and Ganelon. Also those who had told lies and written them in books were hung up by their tongues, Ctesias the historian and Herodotus and Marco Polo and Sir John Mandeville and many others. Then I rejoiced exceedingly knowing I should never come to *that* torment, being by nature truthful and never having written down a false statement in my life. There also I saw a lecturer on physiology pinned out on a table and a frog lecturing upon *him*—the audience was mostly frogs and rabbits. The batrachian Professor was pointing out the disadvantages of a four-chambered heart and the superiority of the batrachian type. Altogether the place was very desolate and struck a chill into my heart—if you want to get an idea of it go to the Imperial Institute and explore the Education Exhibition.

"These are only a few specimens of the wonderful adventures which befell us. How we got back again I do not rightly know."

During the dreary Middle Ages Lucian found no followers—the mediaeval writers did not speak the truth much, being given up to vain imaginations. It is true[1] that Professor Wilamowitz-Moellendorff is of opinion that

[1] As true as the *Vera Historia.*

Dante's *Divine Comedy* is a mediaeval rendering of the *True History*—but I think there are serious difficulties in the way to accepting this view, as there generally are with the literary theories of that distinguished author. With the Renaissance, however, Lucian came back with a bound. The greater part of the amazing book which goes under the name of *Pantagruel* is directly inspired by Lucian. Rabelais, however, though a much smaller artist, was a much greater man than Lucian, and what in the Greek is only an amusing skit becomes in the Frenchman a fierce satire. The voyage of Panurge to seek the oracle of the Divine Bottle starts with no apparent meaning, but gradually it becomes more and more evident that the writer is inditing a parable of the vanity of human endeavours to solve the riddle of existence, to which the final answer is the Epicurean command "Drink"; and in particular it is a furious attack upon the Roman Catholic Church and the corruptions of society. Swift took up the same strain in *Gulliver's Travels*. Coleridge defines Swift as the spirit of Rabelais dwelling in a dry place; the satire in him is not bedewed with the juices of the Divine Bottle, but is fifty times more fierce and misanthropical, attacking not abuses nor religion, but the very nature of man. But Swift also went back to Lucian— especially in the voyage to Laputa, a good deal of which is a direct paraphrase of the Greek. Cyrano de Bergerac also, who has been lately resuscitated upon the stage, imitated Lucian in his fabulous voyage to the Moon—Swift is said to be more indebted to Cyrano than to Lucian himself. Lastly, the adventures of Tom in Kingsley's fascinating *Water Babies* are a softened copy of Rabelais, with the Epicureanism taken out and a gentle and charming light of Christianity diffused over everything. But I do not know that there is any evidence that Kingsley ever so much as read Lucian.

However, the most truly Lucianic of all the moderns is unquestionably Voltaire. With him we began and with him we must end. He also, it must be admitted, was a greater man than Lucian, but there can hardly be said to be any difference in kind—he is Lucian raised to a higher power—though a punster might say that they are both noted for speaking very disrespectfully of higher powers. I do not know that I ever observed any direct imitation of Lucian in Voltaire—he has never adopted his methods nor copied his jests. But both are typical mockers and scoffers. Like his predecessor, Voltaire never wearies of jeering at the established official religion of his time, and at the philosophers; he gibes at them in serious tragedies *à la* Euripides, in mock tragedies such as his *Saul*, in tales and romances, in poems, in his Oceanic correspondence. When Voltaire profanely makes one of his characters say "The scape-goat will serve as an expiation; we will send him into the desert, charged with the sins of the company; he is accustomed to this ceremony, which does not do him the slightest harm, and one understands that anything can be expiated by a goat taking a walk," when we hear that Zadig "knew of metaphysics what has been known in all ages, that is to say precious little," we hear again the voice of Lucian raised against the religion and the philosophy of his age. Only in Voltaire it is refined and sharpened to an inconceivable point; never had any man such an instinct for hitting the nail on the head. In their style also is an extraordinary resemblance—both are swift and clear

P 8

without a superfluous word, both stick to one thing at a time and refuse to be diverted from their purpose by any alluring digressions, both are full of idiom. I speak of their prose, of course, for of Voltaire's tragedies the less said the better, Lucian would have laughed them to scorn—on the other hand, Voltaire's poems are another point which he scores over his rival, and on the whole Voltaire also is a much bigger man.

For indeed Lucian was not a great man, and that is the true reason why he is so much neglected in this busy world. He is an agreeable and amusing jester, but that is all, and there is no weight behind him such as there is with Rabelais and Swift and to a less degree even with Voltaire. And he lived in an age devoid of politics, where the established religion was an empty form, and the new ones were not yet taken seriously in literary circles, an age of emptiness and decay upon the whole, and he suffers accordingly—Aristophanes himself could not have made anything great in those days.

CERVANTES

(Literary Society, 1916)

Cervantes

SOME people say that centenaries are nuisances, that there is no reason why you should make a fuss about a man precisely one hundred years after his birth or death any more than at any other time, and that such celebrations are mostly run in the interests of some noisy modern who is really rather celebrating himself. There is some truth in this, and certainly there is no justification for neglecting the great works of literature for the other ninety and nine years that you may gush about them in the hundredth. But alas! the flesh is weak, and the circulating library is strong, and centenaries have a real value for us in sending us back from our contemporaries to the eternal, from twaddly novels to the *Divine Comedy*, from Arnold Bennett to Cervantes.

This particular year of grace happens to be the ter-centenary of the death of three of the very greatest men upon record; I need not say that I refer to Shakespeare, Cervantes and Iyeyasu. Now there are very good reasons why I should not talk to-day about Iyeyasu, which reasons I had rather not specify but will leave to your imagination. As for Shakespeare you are all sick to death of him, or if you aren't it must be the fault of your English staff. But Spanish literature is sadly neglected in England, a proof of which is that I should have the impudence to get up and talk about it, and Cervantes is the one supremely great name in it.

Miguel de Cervantes Saavedra—how lovely these Spanish

names are—came of a noble and ancient family, which is traced back to the mountainous wilds of Galicia in N.W. Spain, but which had flourished for generations in Castille. His life extends exactly over the period from the death of Henry VIII to the death of Shakespeare, and so his dates are easy to remember, 1547 (29th September)–1616. For the honour of giving him birth seven cities have contended, as seven cities did over Homer, one with a lovelier name than another, but the prize has been given, like the apple of Paris, to the loveliest of them all, Alcalá de Henares. That must be a place worth being born in. About his childhood and education little enough is clear and none of it matters: he certainly knew Latin to some extent, rather a small extent I fancy, and Italian; I do not know that he ever shows any knowledge of French, but he must have picked some up, one would think, in his adventures; he certainly never could have taken a degree in this University, but what graduate of this University ever did anything worth looking at? People of a superior and academic turn of mind sneered at Cervantes in his own day because of his want of learning, exactly as Ben Jonson did at Shakespeare and other folk at Dickens. But what *did* matter about all these people was that they had come in contact with all sorts and descriptions of men and had the eye of genius for understanding and reproducing them, not to say for greatly improving them. After his years of learning Cervantes spent his years of wandering in a school which certainly was not lacking in variety and adventure. He went on different journeys to the South of France and Italy in the retinue of an ambassador, enlisted as a soldier in the ranks and fought at the great battle of Lepanto. The excitement and enthusiasm caused by that campaign is not now so very easy to understand: enough for our purpose that the Venetians were fighting the Turks, who had attacked Cyprus; the Venetians called on the other nations of Christianity to take part in a Crusade against the infidel. Don John of Austria, son of the Emperor Charles V, led the Christian fleet and won a great victory over the Turks at Lepanto on the west coast of Greece in 1571, the year before the massacre of St Bartholomew, an event which throws a lurid light on the union of the Christians against the infidel. In that battle Cervantes fought as a common soldier; though ill of a fever he refused to stay in bed; he distinguished himself by the most daring valour, and received three wounds, two in the body, and the third disabled his left hand for the rest of his life. As he put it himself, he lost his left hand for the greater glory of the right, and he never wearied of referring to the great battle. What he got by it all was three crowns in addition to his pay. The remuneration is characteristic. After some further stay in the Mediterranean he was sent back to Spain in 1575 with letters of recommendation, which turned out ill for him; for he was taken prisoner by the Algerine pirates and carried off to Algiers. There he remained captive five years. The story of the Christian captives in those parts is a horrible one which I need not here go into; so far as Cervantes was concerned we have fortunately a great deal of evidence, which is profoundly interesting as showing what manner of man he was, for I will give you a single instance. A plot had been made of which Cervantes was the author and leader, for sixty of the captives to escape, and was on the point of being carried out, when a scoundrel informed the Turkish governor. The governor thought it advisable to dissemble his knowledge for a time that he might catch the Christians in the act and punish them accordingly. But the news got about that the governor knew everything; the captives were in great alarm, and one of them in particular thought that if Cervantes were seized the Turks would compel him by torture to reveal the whole affair and inform against his accomplices. This fellow entreated Cervantes to embark on some ships which were ready to set sail, offering to pay his ransom. Here was a splendid chance to escape out of Hell; did Cervantes jump at it? Not he: he thought it dishonourable to fly from the danger himself and leave his companions in so great a risk; therefore he not only refused the offer, but calmed the fears of the other, telling him that no torture nor death itself would make him betray any one of his companions; sooner would he lay the blame to himself alone to save them all.

Then for the first time we meet Don Quixote, do you know him when you see him? Is that not how Don Quixote would have behaved? Anybody can fight bravely, and the deeds of Cervantes at Lepanto could be matched doubtless by hundreds of others who fought upon that day. But the man who never thought of saving himself, and was ready to risk impalement and anything else on a point of honour; who not only does this but actually makes the other man believe that no torture will wrest the truth from him; that is indeed Don Quixote talking over Sancho Panza. This is only one specimen of his habitual attitude. Why he was not tortured and killed fifty times is a mystery; his companions constantly feared that he would be: he expected it himself more than once. But when it came to the point, he always somehow got off; there was something about him that overawed and imposed upon his brutal gaolers and tyrants. In truth the whole of the story of the captivity reads more like a fairy tale than real life; and if the evidence for it were not so good, it would be scouted frankly as incredible. As it is, it is not possible to understand it in many points; like the greater part of the life of Cervantes it is "wrop in·mystery."

Be all that as it may, he was finally ransomed and restored to Spain in September 1580. During the next three years he continued his adventurous career, but I will not go into details, for they were of no interest in themselves and do not help us to understand him; it is high time to turn to his literary career. In 1585, aged thirty-eight, he published the first part of his *Galatea*, a pastoral romance divided into six books. On the pastoral I shall have more to say later on. I do not mean to read the *Galatea*; I have many other ways to die, and advise you to leave pastorals to rot in their graves. You remember what Horace Walpole said of Sidney's *Arcadia*: "a tedious, lamentable, pedantic, pastoral romance which the patience of a young virgin in love cannot now wade through."

About this time Cervantes married a young lady of nineteen, Doña Catalina de Palacios Salazar y Vozmediano.

He next tried his hand at the drama, which was then just putting forth its earliest blossoms in Spain as it was in England. His Quixotic enthusiasm for whatever he took in hand seems to have persuaded him that he could make a fortune by the drama; that is not strange, but he succeeded in getting managers to bring out his plays, which is stranger. One of them deserves notice, the *Numancia*. This tragedy has a kind of sombre grandeur about it, perhaps one might better call it a stilted sublimity: it deals with the heroic resistance of Numancia to the Romans, when the natives were finally starved out after fighting to the last gasp. It is a very bad play, a very bad play indeed, but there is a thing to be remembered about it which stirs the blood. When the Spaniards were holding Saragossa against the armies of Napoleon, when they like their ancestors were starving and facing overwhelming odds with a heroism which has become proverbial, then this play of *Numancia* was performed in the theatre amid frenzied enthusiasm to the accompaniment of the cannons of Mortier and Lannes. It was probably the first performance of the tragedy for over 200 years, and probably it was the last.

Anyhow as a dramatist Cervantes was promptly drowned by the amazing deluge of Lope de Vega. Zoologists talk of the fecundity of the herring and the oyster, but those interesting quadrupeds fade into insignificance beside the fertility of Lope. It is estimated that he wrote at least twenty million verses; epic poems, comic poems, romances, anything that came in his way; but his fame rests on his dramas, of which he composed at the lowest fifteen hundred.

About the year 1600 he was certainly in prison for a time, nobody quite knows why or where; he had got a small post under the Government and made a mess of his accounts. Legend says that he wrote, or at any rate conceived the idea of Don Quixote in prison; that like so many legends is highly questionable. At any rate in 1605 the first part of the incomparable masterpiece appeared in print, and the name of Cervantes immediately filled the civilised world. Everybody knows the outline of the story and how absurdly simple it is. An elderly gentleman living quietly with his niece and his housekeeper, having nothing much to do but read, has his brain turned by the romances of chivalry, imagines himself to be destined by Fate to restore chivalry and knight-errantry to the world, persuades a rustic named Sancho Panza to follow him as his squire, goes forth accordingly and meets with all sorts of ridiculous adventures, finally recovers his wits and dies, cursing the books of chivalry.

And what *were* these books of chivalry? No one can be expected to read them nowadays unless he is writing a dissertation. I haven't—except one. There *is* one which is pretty well known, Malory's *Morte d'Arthur*. But that I understand to be altogether an unfair example; it is a million miles too good; it is unspeakably tiresome to read through, and most of it is inconceivably silly if you think about it seriously, and it is horribly immoral, but for all that the Arthurian legend is an interesting thing, and the *Morte d'Arthur* contains many very fine passages. But the sort of romance which turned Don Quixote's head was very different. The stories of Amadis of Gaul, Huon of Bordeaux and so on, had not the interest of Arthurian romance because they were merely silly inventions of professed literary people, not the genuine popular tradition. The characters are reputed to be idiotic, their behaviour and adventures on a par with their characters, their morality as bad as Malory's. Yet people read this rubbish by bucketfuls because they had nothing else in

the way of fiction to read and they were so silly themselves
for the most part that they couldn't read anything but
fiction. Nay, in the seventeenth century that divine
creature, our lady of Livry, Madame de Sévigné herself,
reads and delights in the novels of chivalry written by
Mademoiselle de Scudéry: she is a bit ashamed of it as
she confesses, but read them she does in spite of Don
Quixote.

The knight of course has a lady-love, probably somebody
else's wife, he fights giants and other knights and performs
incredible feats of valour, he is beguiled and bamboozled
by enchanters, and he is supposed to ride abroad redressing
human wrong. All these features in him are of course
parodied in *Don Quixote*, not once nor twice, but over and
over again. There is an enormously long novel of George
Meredith called *Evan Harrington*, built entirely upon the
fact that the hero is the son of a tailor, and there is something very funny about being a tailor—you get sick to
death of it before you are half-way through—at least I did.
But somehow you never get weary of the adventures of
Don Quixote, though it is a much longer book than *Evan
Harrington*. What does bore one in it are just those parts
which are *not* on the gibe of knight-errantry. The rest is
eternally amusing, but it is a great deal more than that.

There is a story that King Philip III saw a man with
a book in his hand overcome with inconsumable laughter.
"Either that man is mad," quoth His Majesty, "or he is
reading *Don Quixote*." And that indeed is the first aspect
in which the book presents itself to us. To enjoy it truly
you must do two troublesome things; you must learn
Spanish and you must grow old. But even if you know no

Spanish and even if you are young, you cannot resist its gaiety and absurdity. At the same time those who only want to laugh may quite easily be disappointed in it. I have heard grave persons of taste and education call it "dull." The fact is that much more amusing books have been written since, if by "amusing" you mean provoking laughter. There are numbers of modern French farces which it is hardly possible to get through for sheer laughter —though they have no literary merit to speak of and though in consequence you can hardly read them a second time. *Don Quixote* no longer produces the effect noted by King Philip III. While a book is at the height of its immediate popularity, it is almost certain that it will be producing its effect upon the public by something superficial, something which will not wear well. The public of those days were consumed with laughter, I am afraid, to a very large extent exactly because of the features in the book which now rather repel us. What amused people then was to see somebody whacked with a big stick. That part of the business now repels us—but what still delights us is the grave and serious humour which spreads a serene light over the whole. It may not make us laugh so much as a Parisian farce, but it abides with us, if we are persons of taste, like you and me, and we can go on reading it all our lives. But I tell you again that you won't appreciate it till old age begins to come upon you—suppose you wait to try it, till you are forty—and by that time ten to one that you will not be reading anything but the last new twaddle from Mudie's.

However, here is a bit which I will translate as well as I can—but unfortunately for my present purpose *Don*

Quixote cannot be represented in extracts; it must be taken as a whole. Let us take one specimen, the battle with the sheep. Don Quixote and Sancho having ridden up to the top of a hillock to get a better view, Don Quixote proceeds to hold forth in the following strain: [Part I, chap. 18].

Such is the first aspect in which *Don Quixote* presents itself—as an extremely amusing book. But presently it begins to dawn upon one that it is a great deal more. It is not true, as has been said, that all great authors necessarily become symbolic, but it is true of many and especially of Cervantes. This knight errant going out on his broken-down old horse to conquer giants and overthrow armies is not merely a skit upon the old books of chivalry, such as the adventures of Amadis or the *Morte d'Arthur*; he is also a satire upon every single one of us, for we are all in our humble way Don Quixotes; he is an ironical type of all the proud imaginations of man. He is going to redress human wrong, and what is the result? He sets free a gang of criminals who are being taken to the galleys. He is going to kill a giant, and he is knocked flat by the sails of a windmill. He has a lady-love, the peerless Dulcinea del Toboso, whom he has never seen and who is really nothing but a blowsy farmer's daughter. Well, is not that so with all of us? We set out nothing doubting to become distinguished scholars and are knocked flat in the Matriculation. Don Quixote says it is due to the malignancy of an enchanter; of course it is not his own fault; *we* say that it is the malice of examiners. We set up some imaginary phantom to worship; it may be a young lady or perhaps more likely a young gentleman in khaki; it may be a determination to square the circle or to put a stop to the wicked practice of vaccination, or to persuade the world to believe in spiritualism; and many people go on worshipping such fetishes all their life long. All their efforts prove fruitless, they only get themselves laughed at, but nothing can shake their belief in themselves and their Dulcinea. "My writings," said Pascal, one of the greatest of men, "may be condemned by the Sorbonne, but they are approved in Heaven." On which Voltaire sarcastically commented that in the court of Heaven they had something else to think of than Pascal's writings. And Voltaire himself? is he not as much of a Don Quixote? He wrote bad tragedies all his life and thought them very fine; he preached all sorts of fine things and never dreamt that he was paving the road to the French Revolution, which would have driven him mad with horror. A certain Swedish philosopher wrote a book to prove that the Swedish constitution was impeccable and indestructible. As he was finishing his last chapter some one came and told him that the King had destroyed the constitution with a stroke of the pen. "Sir," said the philosopher, "he may destroy the constitution but he cannot destroy my book." But there is simply no end to the applications that may be made. Dulcinea is peerless: "Deutschland über alles." What the world wants is knights errant: "We Germans are the salt of the earth."

As we have all a Don Quixote inside us, so we all have a Sancho Panza. Sancho is a dull man who has never seen a heavenly vision, who knows which side his bread is buttered, who is an amazing compound of shrewdness and stupidity; he knows very well that Don Quixote is mad, and yet he follows him because he hopes to get something out of him; he sees him battered with blows and he takes good care to keep out of their way himself, and yet he follows at his heels without knowing why. So in every one of us the lower nature is led grumbling after the higher, and the ill-assorted couple jumbles through the chaos of life as it can. But the parable is plainer if we look at the two characters as disjoined from one another. Is not the socialist party in Germany exactly like Sancho? It went grumbling after the military party with a thick bandage over its eyes because in a muddled way it thought it was going to get something; now that it sees its leader thwacked and is itself tossed in a blanket, it begins to reflect what a fool it has made of itself.

Such is the second aspect in which this book reveals itself, a dazzling commentary on human life, so universal in its application that it completely transcends every other novel ever written. And it is all treated with such grave and delicious irony that one never wearies of it. There is nothing like irony for keeping a book green.

But there is one irony upon another in it. In the second part especially it somehow begins to dawn upon us that the madness and misadventures of Don Quixote are wisdom and happiness as compared with this world. That is the third stage of our experience in studying it. Dulcinea may have appeared to Sancho as a blowsy rustic, but which was the happier, Sancho knowing the truth or his master nursing the illusion? As Rostand says in his enchantingly beautiful play:

Le seul rêve intéresse,
Vivre sans rêve, qu'est-ce?
Moi, j'aime la princesse
Lointaine.

And how distant Dulcinea was!

...let us thither, Sancho, for though I but see her, be it through fences, or windows, or openings of doors, or garden grates, this shall I gain—that whatever ray of the sun of her beauty reaches my eyes, it will enlighten my mind and fortify my heart, so that I shall be unique, and without equal in wisdom and prowess.

(Duffield, trans. 1881, vol. II, p. 526.)

All those other people in the book, and there are more than six hundred of them as it is reckoned by the curious, begin to seem like shadows, like people who have somehow missed the only things worth having in life. They may eat more bacon and receive fewer hard knocks, but we begin to look upon them with disdain. And there are times when even the madness of Don Quixote carries all before it and justifies itself. Once at least was he made manifest in the flesh. There sat in a place called Vaucouleurs a battered old captain of the wars, sick at heart, I think, and if he knew his Virgil saying to himself "Una salus victis nullam sperare salutem." And there came and stood before him a peasant girl of seventeen who could neither read nor write, and said to him: "I come to you in the name of God who is my Lord, that you may tell the Dauphin that God will send him succour in the mid Lent. In spite of his enemies he shall be king and it is I who will lead him to be crowned and sanctified at Rheims."

Which is the madder? Don Quixote going forth on Rozinante to deliver the oppressed, or the peasant girl who summoned to battle the shattered and despairing chivalry of France and by faith put to flight the armies of the aliens? Mad as March hares both of them. Nay, we become ashamed of ourselves; why did we begin by thinking it funny to read of Don Quixote's disasters? We begin to think that it wasn't funny at all, but tragic—the eternal tragedy of lofty aims thwarted by the horrible hard facts of life. In fact we fall in love with Don Quixote. There is a story that six people being asked to write down the name of the finest gentleman they knew of, one and all wrote down his name. This feeling culminates when we read the tale of his final overthrow. A certain bachelor of arts, Sampson Carrasco, goes forth to cure him of his madness at the beginning of the second part; he arms himself like a knight and challenges Don Quixote. But unluckily the bachelor gets the worst of it and is overthrown himself, and commanded by the victor to go and yield homage to Dulcinea. After that we hear no more of him for some hundred pages. Then he appears again on the outskirts of Barcelona as Knight of the White Moon.

...Don Quixote commending himself to Heaven with all his heart, and to Dulcinea, as was his custom at the beginning of all the battles which were offered him, turned to take a little more field, for he saw that his adversary had done the same, and, without sound of trumpet or other martial music to give signal for the onset, they both wheeled their horses at the same instant. And as that of the Silver Moon was more swift, he met Don Quixote before he had run a third of his career, and with such great force, that without touching him with the lance—for it appears that he carried it aloft on purpose—he gave Rozinante, and with him Don Quixote, a parlous fall to the ground. Foot-hot he ran to him, and bringing his lance to his visor, he cried:

"Thou art the conquered knight, and even a dead man, unless thou confess to the conditions of our challenge."

Don Quixote, bruised and stunned, without raising his beaver, and as if he spoke from within a tomb, in a sick and feeble voice said: "Dulcinea del Toboso is the most

P   9

beautiful woman of the world, and I the most miserable knight of the earth; nor is it right that my weakness should belie this truth. Strike home, knight, thy lance, and take my life, seeing thou hast taken away mine honour."

(Duffield, trans. 1881, vol. III, p. 639.)

Do you laugh at it or do you cry? Humour seems to me, so far as I can attach any meaning to the word, to be just this in its highest manifestation, that one doesn't know which to do over it. And how thin is this line which divides comedy from tragedy! Treat the irony of fate and of the world in one way and you have Oedipus, in another and you have Don Quixote.

It is because of this approximation of laughter and tears, because of the development of Don Quixote into something higher than he was at the start, that many of his lovers prefer the second part to the first. There are other reasons also. Into the first part Cervantes threw all sorts of things which he had handy, a whole novel of considerable length, the story of the Moorish captive, and so on. Also he yielded to his old fancy for the pastoral, as he had done before in the *Galatea*. Now you may say a great deal for the pastoral in its proper place. The ideal Arcadia invented by Sannazaro, which ran like wild-fire over all Europe, was a very pleasant dream. Shepherds with pretty names hanging odes upon hawthorns and elegies upon brambles, shepherdesses of amazing beauty and simplicity, sheep which apparently can look after themselves, eternal spring and a capacity to live without food, all these make a very pretty picture. And the story of Cardenio and Dorothea is told in such enchanting language that no one can have the heart to be severe on it in itself.

But there is a glaring defect about it; it is utterly out of place. Don Quixote depends for his effect upon being a dreamer brought in contact with the hard facts of life; pastoral is a denial of these facts. To drag the knight and his squire into the midst of it is as if you should plant Sir John Falstaff and Pistol amid the shepherds of *As You Like It*. Just fancy Falstaff listening to the confidences of Orlando, or Pistol weeping over the sorrows of Rosalind. Then too there is another trouble about the pastoral and about Cervantes in general: the ladies are really all too beautiful. They all have red hair and green eyes, and every one of them outgoes her predecessors. When the Moorish lady removes her mask:

> And so she removed it, and disclosed a face so beautiful that Dorothea held her to be more fair than Lucinda, and Lucinda said she was more beautiful than Dorothea; while all those who stood by knew that if any could equal the beauty of these, it was the lady Moor, and there were some who thought she surpassed them in one thing.
>
> (Duffield, trans. 1881, vol. ii, p. 191.)

One phoenix in a nest is very good business, but three phoenixes in one cage are, in vulgar parlance, all my eye.

A third objection to the first part is the amount of buffeting and, to this squeamish age, the sometimes disgusting disasters of the hero. Charles Lamb protested that they pained his heart.

Whether other critics protested at the time, or whether Cervantes criticised himself, I do not know. Certain it is that in the second part he cleared all these things away; there are no irrelevant novels inserted in it, pastorals are only laughed at and the big stick is reduced to a minimum.

Yet we must admit that though the second part is to be held superior for all the reasons here alleged, yet the first part has the most amusing scenes and conversations in it and the events which are most familiar to all the world. What does it matter anyhow? Let us enjoy them both.

But I go back to the point that there are three stages to be gone through, first mere amusement, secondly the feeling of the universal irony as against Don Quixote, thirdly the feeling that after all Don Quixote is worth all the rest of the people and that his madness is nobler than their sense. And I ask a question which has been often put and answered in many ways. What was the object of Cervantes in writing this amazing book?

The answer, I think, is that he went through two and a half of those stages himself. He began the representation of a comic elderly gentleman going off his head and acting the knight errant just as a prodigious lark. Then as he went on the irony of the situation and the way in which it can be allegorically applied to all human life simply forced itself upon him. Finally he, like everybody else, fell in love with his hero. But I much doubt how far he really intended at any time whatever to make his readers understand that the lunacy of Don Quixote is really better than the common sense of the world. I think that it is we, or at any rate some of us, who largely read that into the story. We have no right to do so, you may say; yes, but we have. When a man has created such a portent and has conquered the whole world without knowing it, he has lost his own rights over his own creation; he has lighted a train of gunpowder and the resulting explosion is no business of his, or to express it better he has discovered a new chemical element which produces one result in contact with his own mind and other results which may be quite different in contact with other minds.

It is only fair to say that Cervantes himself gives quite a different account of the matter; he says, if you can believe him, that his object was to destroy the popular romances of chivalry. The last words of the book are "my desire has been nothing else than to bring into the abhorrence of mankind the false and crazy histories and books of chivalry which already go stumbling to their fall because of those of my veracious Don Quixote, and which without any doubt must fall altogether." Some people have taken those assertions very seriously; Mr Duffield's notes are one continued outcry against the immorality and wickedness of those unhappy books, and he really thinks their destruction was the great achievement of his hero. But if that really was the object of Cervantes, one can only say that he was as blind as a bat; Don Quixote *did* destroy them, but if that was all should we now be talking about him? When an author tells you what his object was in writing a poem or a novel, you can bet what you like that he is deceiving you—probably he deceives himself too. Milton said that he wrote *Paradise Lost* to justify the ways of God to men: if so, he was only fit for a lunatic asylum. Cervantes may have *begun* with that intention, but it is obvious that he went on with others—mainly for the sheer joy of creating an enchanted world and because his radiant and delightful character must needs overflow in some way or other.

For that is another great quality of the book, its radiant good humour, its cheerfulness and brightness. There is not a drop of gall or bitterness to be found in it, and this it is which makes one feel how delightful and sunny a nature its author's must have been. Compare his external life with his great contemporary's. Shakespeare was a prosperous stage-manager, he amassed a fortune and bought a country place at Stratford, he brought out his plays before princes, and we know of no particular grievance of his against the world. Cervantes lost a hand, was prisoner in a horrible captivity five years, was a consistent failure in literature till the age of fifty-eight, was a poor man all his life. Yet it was Shakespeare who at one time turned as sour as vinegar and drew a picture of the world as savage almost as Swift's; it was Cervantes who remained as cheerful as Falstaff, as gay as Rosalind, as good-humoured and wise and tolerant as Don Quixote himself. Yes, as wise, for Don Quixote's wisdom, except on one point, is prodigious, and bursts forth in a perennial stream on every subject of conversation that arises, insomuch that all those who hear him marvel. "Your worship," says Sancho on one occasion, "is better fitted for a preacher than for a knight errant." "Knights errant have to know everything," responded Don Quixote, "there was one in past ages who was as ready to deliver a sermon or·an oration as if he had been a graduate in the University of Paris."

But when Don Quixote begins talking there is no end to it, and I must get on.

This book is Cervantes and Cervantes is this book. But he never knew it, the simple old creature. Between the first and second parts he produced his next best work the *Exemplary Novels*. I will only say of them that if they had not been by Cervantes nobody would ever have heard of them. And at his death he was feverishly putting the last touches to a long romance about Persiles and Sigismunda, of which all I know is that I have read an account of the plot and that it must be enough to drive the most enduring of readers into a strait waistcoat. But there is a description of himself in the Prologue to the *Exemplary Novels* which is worth quoting:

He whom you see here with aquiline countenance, chestnut hair, a smooth and open forehead, cheerful eyes, the nose curved but well proportioned, the beard of silver (less than twenty years ago it was of gold), the moustache large, the mouth small, the teeth none the better for wear, since he has only got six and these in bad condition and worse placed since they don't correspond with one another; the body between two extremes, neither great nor small, the colour fresh, rather fair than dark; somewhat bowed in the shoulders, and not very light of foot—this, I say, is the visage of the author of "The Galatea" and "Don Quixote," etc., commonly known as Miguel de Cervantes Saavedra—he was a soldier many years—

and then of course follows a flight of rhetoric about the battle of Lepanto and the victorious banners of the son of that thunderbolt of war, Charles V, of happy memory.

Only one portrait of him exists, and it corresponds much better with the description I have just read than the author's upper and lower teeth did.

But his mind, his character, his real essence is not so easily described as his outward person. The more one gets to know about him the more one sees how closely he is akin to his own masterpiece. He certainly was not mad, not by any manner of means; *he* never saw St Michael appearing to him in a glory and telling him to go on and prosper (and that in spite of the fact that he was born on

St Michael's day), he was never, so far as we know, affected by any such illusion as was Pascal, nor diseased in his nervous system as so many great authors have been, nor is there any shadow of a cloud of melancholy upon him such as we feel brooding over Molière. Clear shining of the sun upon a smiling landscape seems to be the atmosphere in which his spirit moves, a perpetual serene happiness which no external discomforts or disasters can mar. The kingdom of heaven was within him. And so it was with Don Quixote; what did it matter to him what befell his unlucky body? Take away from Don Quixote his delusion and there, I think, is the author himself. As the knight of La Mancha was utterly fearless of all dangers, insomuch that he opened the door of the lions and defied them to come out and fight him, so Cervantes defied his Turkish masters and was ready to face much worse than death without turning a hair. As the former drags Sancho after him, inflaming even that fleshly nature with a spark of his own enthusiasm, so the latter persuaded everybody with whom he came in contact to follow his lead, whether they were captives in Algiers or stage-managers in Spain. But why then did he not prosper better in this world? Because though he was not mad he was nevertheless all in the dark about himself, as so many of these geniuses are. O, the time he wasted over trying to write poetry, and the naïveté with which he palms off his verses upon us! Cervantes had no ear for verse, no instinct for finding anything to say in verse if he could have written it, yet he went on pegging away at it just as Goethe did at his perfectly disgusting attempts at making pictures. He wrote plays by the dozen, and except for the doubtful case of *Numancia* they are failures too. And the pastoral romance hung about his neck like a millstone all his life. And why did he never succeed as a soldier? The answer to that question can only be a guess, but my guess is that he was a great deal too like Don Quixote again. Certainly it was not for lack of valour, but I suspect that he was devoid of the sense of what was practicable and what was not. Alike as soldier and as writer I picture him to myself as moving recklessly in the pursuit of flying stars through a wilderness of bog and brier, never heeding the hard facts of life, never losing heart, never without a smile on his lips at his own misadventures. He looks on the pageant of life around him, and illuminates it all with his own brightness. But to this you must add his delicious humour, a quality in which his hero was perhaps a little deficient. A man with humour in him would certainly never have behaved like a Quixote. But Cervantes had not only a Quixote within him; he had also a Sancho Panza, and we may be sure that he provided his own commentary upon his own extravagances. Indeed you have just heard him do it: the hero who followed the banner of the invincible Don Juan has only six teeth in his head, and they do not correspond.

There out of Cervantes' own lips is the description of the knight errant and the practical remark of the honest and unromantic squire. Indeed there is a passage of which one is irresistibly reminded by this description. Directly after the adventure of the sheep, Don Quixote holds forth on the heroic deeds and wisdom of knights errant and presently adds "but just put your finger in my mouth and see how many teeth are missing on my upper jaw upon the

right, for that is where I feel the pain," the shepherds
having hit him there with a stone from their slings.

I do not know whether I have succeeded in making in
any way clear my notion of the sort of man Cervantes was,
but indeed if you want to get any impression of him worth
having I repeat again that you must learn Spanish and
must grow old, and I know very well that you are im-
mutably determined to do neither the one nor the other.
"Paciencia y barajar," as Durandarte said when he woke up.

JULIAN

Literary Society, 1903)

Julian

THERE is a vast chasm in the knowledge of most of us, a great gulph fixed between the two worlds ancient and modern. The names of Socrates and Caesar, Alexander and Herod the Great, Solomon and Marcus Aurelius are familiar to all even if they be not professed students of antiquity. Greece, Rome and Judaea in a word still live for us. But then comes a great waste chaos lighted by scarce a star; we know that Muhammad and Charlemagne and one or two others are weltering somewhere in it and that is about all. There is indeed a bridge across this chaos. Edward Gibbon, resembling Sin and Death in *Paradise Lost*, and indeed he was as ugly as sin, built that bridge with wondrous art; it stands high, spanning that thousand years more or less; and scarce a brick in the majestic structure shows trace of decay. Everybody must read Gibbon once in his life, but I suppose not many of you have done it yet.

Meantime the last figure which still stands on the shore of that ancient world has still a strange fascination and romance about him. By the triumphant party which he opposed he has been pilloried under the name of apostate, which after all only means a man who has changed his mind. Yet somehow or other the Apostate has remained a far more vivid figure than any of his opponents, however triumphant their cause. More vivid and more romantic. Who knows or cares anything about Ambrose? Ambrose, the author of the greatest of Christian lyrics, reformer of

Church music, priest and statesman, perhaps a greater man
than Julian—he is as dead as last year's cricket averages—
that is to the ordinary reader. He advanced the cause he
had at heart, Julian lost his. Perhaps that is just it. The
descending sun of Rome, and all the glorious memories
evoked by the name of Rome, cast a gleam of light upon
the head of her last defender even as he was swallowed up
in the rising tide, and that last gleam is more pathetic and
more romantic than the blaze of sunshine. The legend
invented against him by his enemies has helped to conse-
crate him, for the picture of the dying warrior crying
"Thou hast conquered, O Galilaean" is as familiar as that
of Alfred burning the cakes, and as moving as the last hour
of Socrates. And it may be added it is equally false—it
shares the fate of so many of those pretty historical
anecdotes, it may have all sorts of merits but its evidences
will not bear inspection. But it shows the fear and hatred
with which the Galilaeans, as he calls them, regarded him,
and it typifies better than anything else the attitude he
bears in history; it is a crowning example of the truth of
Aristotle's profound saying that poetry is truer than history.

On the other hand he has been applauded and be-
herofied in late years by a very different set, by people who
have in their turn apostatised from Christianity and who
think any stick will do to beat a dog with. Their puffing
of Julian is like the pilgrimage to the shrine of Giordano
Bruno which is undertaken every now and then in Rome
simply to annoy the Pope and give the police something
to do. Julian would have given these amiable enthusiasts
as short shrift as he gave the Christians.

For in fact he was an eminently religious person; had

he not been so he never would have apostatised at all. Gallio does not trouble himself in that way, especially when it is tolerably evident that he will be on the losing side.

By the time that Julian assumed the purple and threw off the mask, that surely must have been evident. The edicts of Milan had granted peace and toleration to the Church in the years 311 and 313, the last great persecution in the days of Diocletian having proved a sad failure; Constantine had declared for Christianity himself, and it had become the established religion of the Empire; no calm judge can well have doubted by the time of Julian's birth, about 330, that it had won the day. Julian was the nephew of Constantine and was himself brought up as a Christian—one of his instructors being possibly a bishop. But perhaps this was not much in his favour, for de Quincey has remarked that the sons of bishops are always disagreeable.

Possibly the circumstances of his early life were not calculated to inspire him with a great love for his Christian relatives or great faith in their professions. Julian was about seven years old when Constantine died and was succeeded by his three sons. Their accession was celebrated by a general massacre of all their relatives, which secured their position, and from which Julian only escaped because of his extreme youth. But the whole character and behaviour of his kindred was calculated to fill him with disgust. His cousin Constantius, who reigned more or less alone during the next twenty-four years, was a jealous and contemptible tyrant for whom it is vain to attempt apology. And as for Constantine himself, though we are apt to regard him with reverence as the patron of Christianity, yet a nearer view rubs all the gilt off the gingerbread. Among other trifles he murdered his own son. Even his conversion has been doubted by many writers who think it is no more sincere than that of Henry IV of France. But there is one circumstance which leads me strongly to believe in his sincerity; being precisely that on which many doubts have been founded. He was never baptised till he was on his deathbed. He had been trying a water cure for his body and when that had proved unavailing he took one for his soul instead; it may sound profane to put it in that language, but it is the literal fact; baptism was in those days held to be somehow a passport to Paradise. And in postponing the ceremony to his deathbed Constantine resembled many other persons of the time. Baptism absolved you of all past sins, but not of any in which you might indulge after it, and if you felt a strong presumption that you would indulge in them pretty freely (as Constantine must have done) it was as well to wait. Such was the orthodox view. But suppose now that Constantine was *not* sincere and consider the natural course for him to take. Surely he would have got baptised at once to show that he really was a Christian. To defer it was bad policy because it would infallibly give rise to those very doubts about his sincerity which *have* arisen, and if as a matter of policy he wished to be thought one, clearly he would have got baptised at once. Therefore I hold that his conversion was perfectly genuine—why not? It is unfortunately only too certain that a genuine belief in any religion may go along with crimes innumerable.

But this is a digression. Anyhow Julian had good enough reason to doubt the moral value of Christianity—the difficulty rather is to know why he should have been so enthusiastic in favour of Paganism. That was neither moral, nor up to date, nor the winning side—so at least it appears to us from our point of view. But though we think of Paganism as a whole as immoral, yet it proved capable of satisfying the moral sense of eminently moral men and men of the very first intellect. Hostile criticism of it there had been in plenty before any thought of abolishing it had arisen. The criticism had caused thinking men with moral and religious tendencies to read new meanings into the old texts. They interpreted them to suit their own convictions when they could no longer swallow their literal statements. So all the Homeric figures became to them allegories—Jupiter was the aether, or the creative force of nature, or the Sun. If he quarrelled in a most unseemly manner with his wife, and kicked his son out of heaven, that forsooth was only a way of explaining or disguising some natural phenomenon or inculcating some profound religious maxims—what particular one you liked to choose was your own affair. Above all, the old Greek and Roman pantheon had been enlarged to make room for an Oriental deity who had become of the highest importance in the eyes of mystics of that date. His name was Mithras, and he started life in Persia as a personification of sunlight. Gradually he became more and more important, and was taken into partnership with the strange group of metaphysical abstractions, emanations and the like, which were talked about by the neo-Platonists. He is closely connected with the Sun, but in the opinion of the more elevated philosophers, such as Julian, was by no means to be identified with him.

To go into the bastard system of metaphysics and religion would only bore you, even if I could understand it
sufficiently myself to make it intelligible. One of the
principal authorities is Julian's own oration on the subject,
which I can honestly recommend anyone whatever to flee
from as the plague.

The *Orations* are the earliest in date, the most elaborate,
and the most tiresome of all the works of our author. They
do not redound to his credit. The first especially is a rather
shameful performance. It is an elaborate and monstrously
highflown panegyric of that very Constantius who was the
Emperor, being Julian's cousin, and of whom I have had
to speak in very uncomplimentary language before. But
Julian was in an awkward place. He was of course celebrated for his learning, for his love of poetry and rhetoric,
for his literary capacity. At the same time he was a near
relation and at the Emperor's mercy. It is rather a wonder
that he was spared at all, and he certainly would not have
been if he had ventured to reveal his real sentiments.
Consequently he was forced into an abject hypocrisy in
every word and act. Of course he *might* have acted openly,
he might have said to his cousin that he did not feel capable
of giving him a testimonial which after all would be no use,
he might have said in like manner that he found it no
longer possible to believe in Christianity. We know of
plenty of men in history who would have done so—and
there were plenty of men then living who would have de-
clined to abjure their religion, plenty who if they had been
converts to Christianity would have said so even if the
result had been martyrdom. But who will be a martyr for
a metaphysical abstraction?—for the flimsy relics of a soap-

bubble, even if it be as gaudily coloured as neo-Platonism was by its rhetorical professors? Anyhow, one can't help agreeing with Gibbon that this oration is equally disgraceful to both parties concerned. Constantius is compared in it and preferred for genius and morals to Alexander the Great, Agesilaus and other heroes of the past, he is a finer fellow than Achilles, a greater orator than Demosthenes, his magnificence, temperance (good Heavens!), eloquence, military skill and clemency to the vanquished are all remarkable.

No sooner was Julian himself Emperor and his lamented cousin dead, than the tune changed. In an elaborate epistle to the Council and People of Athens, Julian defended his conduct and spoke out what he thought about Constantius. "This most humane of princes," he says with bitter scorn, "murdered without trial six of his own cousins and mine, and my father who was his own uncle; as for me and my brother, he wished to kill us, but ended by banishing us instead."

One observes that he is not content with facts but imputes to his enemy evil thoughts besides. How could he know the secret wishes of Constantius? If Constantius wished to kill him why didn't he? This habit of pushing your points to the utmost, of exaggerating wherever it is to your interests to do so, of making out your own case to be better than it really is and your adversary's worse than it really is—all this is unfortunately a characteristic of Greek generally—at any rate from the fifth century B.C. onwards. The habit of turning everything into a field for rhetorical discussion, a subject for a debating society, is one that is very tempting to an acute mind, and the Greeks were acute beyond any other nation. They loved to debate questions themselves, they loved to hear others debating them too, alike in the public assembly, in the law court, in tragedy or comedy, at a drinking party—in short all day and every day.

If this habit is discernible in the great authors of the past, when all the free states of Greece were flourishing and life was more fully life indeed than it has ever been since, how much more deplorable did it become when the Roman Empire had crushed everything under its level uniform weight and political life was utterly extinct! The degenerate Greeks went on arguing and debating—if they could no longer shake the arsenal and fulmine over Greece, they could at least go on inventing sham speeches to put into the mouths of historical characters—much as if we nowadays were to amuse ourselves with publishing imaginary addresses by William the Conqueror to his troops before Hastings. In this artificial dead wearisome school of rhetoric Julian was brought up; he was himself a type of the argumentative chattering Graeculus of the decadence if ever there was one. When he sits down to compose an oration in praise of his deadly enemy or to defend his action in rebelling against the same enemy, you feel all the time that it really doesn't much matter which he is doing, that he is really interested in putting literary touches to his work, not in the work itself—that he wants to show how clever a fencer he is according to the rules. You don't feel that with a great orator. The result accordingly of reading these works is extreme depression and a sort of nervous irritation.

Still worse are his rhapsodies about Mithras and Atys,

emanations and essences and existences. For not only do they ring insincere but they are mainly unintelligible.

You may feel inclined by this time to ask: Why then trouble oneself about Julian at all? How can anybody think him a great man in any way? What has he to do with literature? And yet in his way he *was* a great man. As such he impressed the most impartial and keenest-sighted of his contemporaries, the historian Ammianus Marcellinus. For he was fortunate in this also, that his life is recorded by a great historian, one who if compared with the other historians of the Empire after Tacitus, is a perfect giant, and who will indeed bear comparison with any Roman historian whatever. At least he is incomparably the most impartial and honest among them all. So much is this the case that it has always remained uncertain whether he was or was not a Christian, though for my own part I have no doubt whatever that he was *not*. Though Julian is his great hero, he never shrinks from blaming him when he thinks him wrong. But his style is generally deplorable, he tries to be fine, and isn't; he indulges in foolish and unintelligible speculations about rainbows; people call him turgid and coarse and other pretty epithets; he came too late and so is ignored by classical scholars, though I *have* seen a piece of him set for translation in the M.A. He was a good soldier and a man of sense.

There can be no sort of doubt about the impression Julian made upon *him*. He cannot have cared a straw about his neo-Platonism nor about his rhetoric, and he did not approve of his attitude towards the Christians. But it is plain all through that he thinks Julian the one great man of his time—he speaks of him as Milton spoke of Cromwell. And the one passage in which his swelling efforts to reach the sublime are for once successful, is that in which he recounts the elevation of Julian to the Caesarship.

For Constantius after massacring nearly all his relations found himself at last in a fix which was common to Roman Emperors of those times. The Empire was so unwieldy and unmanageable that one man could not look after it. This led them time after time to try experiments in the way of dividing it, but these divisions made things worse because the rival rulers sooner or later always flew at one another's throats. Constantius, feeling the necessity for devolving some part of the government on another, accordingly looked about him for a partner, for there were threatening clouds all round the horizon, and he had no son of his own to succeed him. Indeed, owing to his own thoughtful measures, he had no relations at all by this time except Julian. So he took the astounding and desperate step of giving Julian the title of Caesar. This was not equivalent to Emperor, but a sort of Prince of Wales.

Julian at this time was studying philosophy and literature at Athens, the city he loved best in the world. He had a great reputation among the students there, the sort of reputation of a senior wrangler; nobody thought of him as anything but a hard-working devotée of literature. Probably Constantius thought such a man was safe enough and would give him no trouble, but if so what was the good of making him Caesar? It is a hopeless puzzle.

Julian obeyed the summons with great reluctance. He was leaving his books and everything he valued, and for what? He came to Milan and there with great pomp and magnificence was endued with the purple, which in his eyes

was but too ominous. It was Nov. 6th, 855. As the
soldiers clashed their shields upon their knees and broke
into applause, the new Caesar repeated to himself the line
of Homer, "Purple death and violent fate seized him."
He departed for Gaul, and in a few months the world was
filled with his renown.

There does not seem to be any parallel in history for the
change. This awkward long-legged student, with his eager
restless way of walking, his nervous excitable outbursts
of talking, his loud undignified laughter, his silly rhetorical
school exercises, who had been heard to murmur "O Plato"
as he practised the goose-step after his promotion, who had
mourned at having to shave off his philosophical beard and
adopt the soldier's coat for the student's gown—this
Brutus suddenly threw off the mask and appeared as the
greatest warrior of his age. Though his inexperience, and
a rashness which never deserted him and finally ruined
him, caused him some sound losses at first, yet in 857 he
won a great victory over the German invaders of Gaul at
Strasburg. His administration of Gaul, both civil and
military, was in the highest degree practical and successful.
He lived like an ascetic or a Stoic, refusing to have a fire
in the coldest winter, eating little, sleeping less, sitting up
all night to compose some literary performance and working
all day at the business of the Empire.

There is no time to go into the final quarrel with Constantius which led to Julian becoming Emperor. Enough
to say that he was blameless, that the soldiers got excited
and alarmed, and insisted on their beloved general assuming
the sovereignty. One night he was awakened by the din
of armour and the cry of "Julian Augustus," a cry which

was treason. He vainly tried to pacify the soldiers—they broke in and raised him on a shield, and a standard-bearer placed his military collar on his head as a crown. Julian, for whatever reason, yielded—some said in fear of his life— he himself said to prevent anyone else being made Emperor, but that I cannot believe.

Constantius might have accepted the elevation, irregular as it was, and the two emperors might have reigned together. But he was already consumed with jealousy and hatred of his rival, and refused to recognise him. Civil war was assured. But neither party was in a hurry to begin— both in the East and West their hands were full, campaigning against enemies of the Empire. When Julian did at last strike, he struck like lightning. The military situation will be most easily imagined by you if you suppose a small army throwing itself with inconceivable rapidity from Paris upon Vienna, and supposing it to have taken Vienna it has then got to attack a superior force and make its way through immensely difficult country to Constantinople. This bare sentence shows the enormous difficulty of Julian's undertaking, one which he could have hardly ventured on perhaps, if he had not expected and had not hoped for treason on the other side. He may well have had reason to believe that he would be welcomed in the East.

Anyhow, he carried out the first part of the programme in so masterly a manner that one is irresistibly driven to think of the similar campaign of Napoleon in 1805. Julian from Paris, Napoleon from Boulogne, advanced in one case on Sirmium in the other on Vienna (it comes to the same thing) with a wonderfully similar series of converging columns and with the same amazing rapidity which completely threw their enemies into bewilderment. But one cannot help observing that Napoleon risked nothing and Julian risked everything. His reckless audacity, however, served him well—everywhere he was successful, and was welcomed by admiring crowds in Sirmium itself, then one of the great ganglions of the Empire. Then he halted and just at the nick of time Constantius had grace enough to die—nothing in his life became him like the leaving of it— he could not have better timed his exit from the stage. By this "crowning mercy" Julian found himself in 361 sole master of the Roman world.

His next two winters were passed at Constantinople and Antioch. Amid the enormous labours of reform of various kinds, and the administration of the over-swollen Empire, he found time to write his three most celebrated and principal works—and others besides for that matter.

These were first a treatise against the Christians which has naturally perished and is only known in fragments from those who again wrote against it, secondly the *Caesars* and thirdly the *Misopogon*. He wrote with amazing swift- ness—as he did anything else—and one is astounded to hear that some of his orations were composed in a single night.

The *Caesars* is a prose satire written at Christmas-time A.D. 362. The plot is thus. Romulus invites the gods and the Roman Emperors to a banquet—the gods take their places first and watch the entry of the Caesars one by one. The drunken and bloated Silenus, companion of Bacchus and a sort of Falstaff of mythology, acts the part of jester, and it is his satirical and comic remarks that are the real essence of the piece. Julius Caesar came first and is taunted

with his ambition. Then Augustus, changing colour like
a chameleon, first making up to Venus and the Graces and
then handed over by Apollo to Zeno the Stoic philosopher,
who turns him out a decent and respectable member of
society. Every one of them is gibed at for some defect
except Julian's great model Marcus Aurelius—and even
he is reproached for his indulgence to his good-for-nothing
wife and son. When all the company are assembled, a
competition is started between Julius, Augustus, Trajan
and Alexander the Great to decide which is the greatest
hero—Marcus Aurelius is also thrown in to represent
philosophy—and Constantine is allowed to go in, really in
order that Julian may make an attack upon his character
and his religion. After they have all made speeches for
themselves, the gods award the palm, as you might expect,
to Marcus the Philosopher, but each of these heroes is
allowed to choose a special patron among the gods that he
may not depart unhonoured. Alexander chooses Heracles
and Trajan runs after Alexander, Augustus takes Apollo,
Marcus Jupiter and Saturn, Julius Caesar Mars and
Venus. But Constantine, says the writer, "not finding
among the gods the pattern of his own life, spied out
Luxury and ran to her, and she embracing him and decking
him up in fine raiment took him to Profligacy—and then
he found Christ wandering about and proclaiming to all:
"Whoever is a corrupter of others and guilty of blood-
shedding, accursed and abominable, let him come with
boldness, for with this water I will wash him and make him
clean, and if he again fall into the like iniquity, I will grant
unto him to become clean by just striking his breast and
beating his head." And Constantine met with him gladly

and departed, he and his sons, from the assembly of the gods. But nevertheless did the avenging furies make havoc of him for his godlessness, exacting vengeance of him for shedding of kindred blood, until Zeus granted him a respite for the sake of his ancestors. As for Julian, he is dedicated by Mercury to Mithras.

I have read this passage because it is the most illuminating of all Julian's written words. The first thing that must strike you on hearing it is the singular and unexpected fact that what Julian blames in Christianity is not lack of evidence for the doctrines nor the ruin it was sure to bring on the ancient life he loved—not what you would expect at all—but its immorality. Astonishing indeed must that seem to us, in whose ears have rung so long that appalling denunciation of the Greek and Roman world in the first chapter of St Paul's Epistle to the Romans. Astonishing to all classical students who have investigated the sink of iniquity into which the Roman Empire had sunk by the time that the leaven of Christianity entered into it, who have read their Petronius (which *I* haven't), their Juvenal and their Tacitus. All the more remarkable for us to be waked up to consider this passage; written by a man whose own morality was blameless and who believed himself even more superior than he was. How blind even the wisest among us are to the great stream in which we move! especially how blind is the Pharisee to human life! And the Pharisee is as rampant now as ever he was.

That is the second point—that Julian was a Pharisee of the strictest sect. Outside his own Little Bethel of Mithras and moonshine there was no salvation, and he thanked Mithras that he was not as other men. And with that forsooth he was going to convert the world and dam up the torrent of Christianity. Here is a specimen of his religion for you, a prayer addressed to the Mother of the Gods. "O mother of gods and men, that sittest enthroned with mighty Zeus, O fountain of the divine intelligence, companion of the pure essences of the intelligible gods, that hast received the common cause of all things from all and dost give them to the divine intelligences, mother of life, Wisdom, Providence, Creatress of our souls, thou that lovest the great Dionysus and didst save Attis when he was cast forth and bring him back when he entered into the abyss of earth, thou who leadest the divine intelligences in the path of all good things and fillest the visible world therewith and hast granted of thy munificence all good things to us in all."

I should think that is enough of it. There is not much immorality about that, and it must be a great comfort to the unhappy and the weary, and all those that seek to cast their burdens upon some divine helper. It is as bad as the Athanasian Creed. "Come unto me all ye that labour and are heavy laden and I will give you rest." But that, we see, was an abomination to Julian—the sinner was *not* to be cleansed and there was to be no redemption for him. And he is surely, we may hope, unfair in suggesting that the Christians of his time did not insist upon repentance and a better life. Of course the case of Constantine himself, with his baptism deferred to his deathbed that he might sin at leisure and repent in haste—that was enough to cause a scandal. But it is a pity that kings and emperors should be expected to live virtuously or decently—Julian is really unconscionable.

But what astonishes me most is that this passage should have been handed down to us at all—what were the Christians who transcribed it thinking about?

The *Misopogon* or *Beard-Hater* is an extraordinary production which Julian composed at Antioch while there engaged in preparation for his great enterprise against Sapor, the famous King of Persia. The people of Antioch and Julian could not get on together at all. Most of them were Christians, divided into three sects who quarrelled with one another as bitterly as if they had had an Education Bill before them. The Pagans were a luxurious and idle lot, caring for nothing but games and shows. Julian despised all parties and all parties hated Julian. The Christians hated him as an Apostate to their religion, the Pagans because he was too superior and philosophical—Julian was disgusted with them also because they didn't even keep up the Pagan religion respectably. He went to a temple to celebrate a great festival, expecting a multitude of votaries and rich sacrifices—he met one priest bringing a goose provided at his own expense.

A dignified prince would certainly not have condescended to take any notice of the rabble who laughed at him and misunderstood him. But Julian's dignity was a frightful minus quantity, and it is evident that he had vanity enough to make him smart under the annoyance of the flies who stung him into angry retort. This it is which makes one feel a painful littleness about him, that makes a strange mixture with his great qualities.

The title *Beard-Hater* is due to the beard being regarded as the sign of a philosopher. Julian cherished as fine a beard as he could grow as the external and visible sign of his calling. This was apparently most unorthodox for a general or a ruler, and afforded a handle for the laughter of the satirical populace.

But the Emperor could hold his own in the domain of satire. The *Misopogon* is written from the point of view of the inhabitants of Antioch who hate beards—i.e. hate all philosophy and culture; with elaborate irony Julian attacks and ridicules himself, jeering at everything of which he was really proud. This irony is so elaborate that it has deceived many people in later times and most extraordinary to tell, even the great master of irony, Gibbon himself. Here is a specimen:

I cannot flatter myself that my countenance is peculiarly beautiful or comely to look upon, but so boorish and un-polished am I that I have made it worse by the addition of this thick beard, punishing it, it seems, purely and simply for not being beautiful. That is why I put up with—er—insects which run about it like animals in a forest.

Gibbon has positively been deceived by this into talking of Julian's being proud of the size and populousness of his beard!

In reality the whole piece is a bitter attack upon the luxury, the utter absence of any intellectual life, and the general degradation of the Antiochenes, and a lofty defence of himself; and it ends up with the ominous words: "Hence-forth I will try to be wiser in my conduct towards you, and may the gods give you the fit reward for your benevolence to me and the public honour you have done me."

Besides these two satires, the letters are worth reading; nothing ever throws so much light upon a man as his correspondence, and luckily a great deal of Julian's is preserved. They show him in all sorts of lights, as a lofty, noble and amiable man in his intercourse with the chosen few, as an intolerant despiser of the multitude.

To Ecdicius, prefect of Egypt.

Though you write to me on no other subject, you ought at least to have written concerning that enemy of the gods, Athanasius, especially as you have long been acquainted with our edicts against him. I now swear by the great Serapis that if the enemy of the gods does not leave Alexandria, or rather Egypt, before the calends of December, the officers of your government shall be fined a hundred pounds of gold. You know my temper: I am slow to condemn, but I am slower still to forgive. (*Postscript in autograph*) His contempt for all the gods fills me with grief and indignation. Nothing that you can do will give me so much pleasure as to hear that the abominable Athanasius, who has presumed in my reign to persuade several Greek ladies of rank to be baptised, is expelled from all Egypt. (Epistle VI.)

It was at this time, while the Emperor was in the full flush of his prosperity, engaged in preparations for the overthrow of Persia, rebuilding the temple at Jerusalem, and finishing off Athanasius, that the famous oracle came to him from Delphi, whither he had sent to enquire of Apollo. The temple was destroyed and the vale of Castaly was desolate, but somehow an answer was given.

Go ye and tell the Emperor that the carved work of the sanctuary is cast down upon the ground, and the god thereof hath no longer where to lay his head. And the laurel of his divination is withered, and the waters that spoke with voices are dried up.

"A strange coincidence!" writes Myers in one of those purple patches of which he was so fond, "that from that Delphian valley, whence as the legend ran had sounded the first of all hexameters—the call as in the childhood of the world to 'birds to bring their feathers and bees their wax' to build by Castaly the nestlike habitation of the young new-entering god—should issue in unknown fashion the last fragment of Greek poetry which has moved the hearts of men, the last Greek hexameters which retain the ancient cadence, the majestic melancholy flow."

With this ominous answer and no other from any oracle of the dead gods Julian set forth on his great enterprise. But his rashness this time was not condoned by Fortune. He got to Ctesiphon indeed on the Euphrates, but found it necessary to retreat, over a desert country, in want of supplies, harassed incessantly by an active and pertinacious enemy. Even so he still devoted his nights to study and meditation. On his last night we are told the Genius of the Empire appeared to him (not for the first time), but now covered with a funeral veil and retreating from him—he leapt up and stepping out into the cool night saw a blazing meteor shoot across the sky and vanish. In the morning as he led the van of his army he heard that the Persian horse had attacked the rear—he seized a shield and hastened to their relief; the attack became general, but was repelled, and as Julian on horseback led the pursuit, calling on his troops and exposing himself with reckless valour, under the burning sun and amid a whirlwind of sandy dust and stamping chargers, he was struck by a flying javelin in the side, and fell from his horse. The victory of the Romans was complete, but the soul of their army lay dying in his tent.

His death is compared to that of Socrates—Ammianus puts into his mouth a philosophical discourse the authenticity of which is doubtful to say the least, but it is certain that he passed his last hours in conversing with two philosophers on the nature of the soul. He died without pain about midnight, June 26th, 363.

And then falls the curtain of history upon living men, at least in Europe, not to rise again till that day in 1274 when in Florence appeared to Dante that Beatrice of whom he was to write things never before written of mortal woman, clothed in a most noble colour, girt and adorned as became her tender years. In all the 900 years before is nothing but ghosts and shadows moving in the mist, and "in all the endless roads they tread there's little but the night." They have fine names, some of them wore crowns, and some were great saints and great men of all kinds, St Louis and Alfred, Benedict, Charlemagne, Theodoric, Stilicho—but there is not one whom I feel that I know or care about. But Julian is a man whom we *can* know, one whom in spite of his errors we can admire and even love. Had he fallen on happier times he might have been among the principal names of either history or literature, and even as it is he is quite worth reading and studying.

THE RELATIONS OF POETRY AND SCIENCE

(Literary Society, 1912)

The Relations of Poetry and Science

IT is a common opinion, I believe, that poetry and science are antipathetic things, and this opinion may be bolstered up by quotations from representatives of both Faculties, if I may so call them. I have long thought myself that this opinion is, however, one which has been very hastily formed, that there is no real evidence to be adduced in its support, that the evidence is in fact the other way round. That is to say, that the poetic and scientific types of mind are by no means mutually exclusive, but touch on one another in many points, and though it is true that excessive addiction to either pursuit will probably render the mind incapable of the other, yet the two will run very well in harness.

It is just as well to begin by defining one's terms—one of the principal reasons for the deplorable nature of most literary discussion is the neglect to begin by doing this. Consequently, as the brothers de Goncourt observed, it almost invariably degenerates into the position "My taste is better than yours"—either asserted boisterously or hinted under a pretence of modesty. Then people begin to raise their voices and get red in the face and make themselves ridiculous.

But in literature one cannot define one's terms with mathematical accuracy any more than one can in ethics. Different people have very different notions about what they mean by poetry, and nobody need quarrel with his neighbour's using it in any sense that seems good to him, if only he will state as clearly as possible to begin with what that sense is. So for the purpose of this present paper I declare that by poetry I mean any good literature written in verse and not prose. That I take to be more or less the sense in which the word is understood by the general public in England, and though in German and in Cherokee the word may cover different ground, I am neither a Cherokee nor a German myself, and have a very absurd and unreasonable fancy for talking plain English. And by science I mean what is commonly understood as natural science, exclusive of mathematics and the application of science to practice.

Certainly nobody will suggest that poets are given to mathematics. I can only think of one instance of their combination in the same individual, Omar Khayyám, who was, I believe, a great mathematician for his age and country, and who reformed the calendar of Persia, even as he says himself:

> Ah, but my Computations, People say,
> Reduced the Year to better reckoning? Nay,
>   'Twas only striking from the Calendar
> Unborn To-morrow, and dead Yesterday.

It is true that the peculiar merit of Manilius, according to his latest editor, who certainly knows plenty about poetry, consists in his skill in doing arithmetical sums in verse, but Manilius does not come under the head of "good literature in verse," and is so ruled out by my definition.

But when we turn to the other sciences, we find quite a different story to tell. It is true that certain poets have lent their aid to foster the popular belief; two of the greatest poets of the last century in England have perhaps done so more vehemently than any others. I mean, of course, Wordsworth and Keats. Wordsworth is eternally declaring in good verse and in bad verse alike that you ought to open your mouth and shut your eyes and ask no questions.

> Enough of science and of art;
>   Close up these barren leaves;
> Come forth, and bring with you a heart
>   That watches and receives.

It was this attitude of mind that so much allured Matthew Arnold. A. C. Bradley has fallen foul with justice of Arnold's famous lines at Wordsworth's grave:

> The cloud of mortal destiny,
> Others will front it fearlessly—
> But who, like him, will put it by?

"Shut his eyes to human trouble?" cries Bradley indignantly—"not he," and he produces a multitude of instances to the contrary where Wordsworth has painted in blackest colours the misery of life. Very true, and yet what Arnold says is true too. Wordsworth knew well enough that the world was full of affliction, and did not attempt to forget it, but what he *did* attempt to escape from was the scientific spirit, which enquires into things. That is the real moral of that remarkable poem the *Advice to Fathers*. It is true that he heads the poem by a pretence that it has a different moral, that it is intended to show how easily the habit of telling lies may be implanted in the youthful mind. But that, as Charles Lamb would have said, "was only his fun." You all remember how the father worries the unhappy child to tell him why he likes one place better than another,

> And five times to the child I said,
> "Why, Edward? tell me why."

At last the unhappy infant, goaded to desperation by his tormentor, answers that it was because there is a weather-cock at one place and none at the other, and the poet lifts his eyes to Heaven and thanks his Creator for teaching him so many lessons at the hands of babes and sucklings. But what *was* the lesson? Not, as he says, that the habit of lying may easily be taught, but that you ought to enjoy Nature and not go grubbing up the reasons for it. Accept the simple impressions of things upon your mind, and do not investigate them scientifically. One might quote fifty poems to illustrate the same thing; I content myself with one pyramidal example:

> One impulse from a vernal wood
> May teach you more of man,
> Of moral evil and of good,
> Than all the sages can.

That is to say that you learn more about virtue and vice, and the true end of human life and so on, by lying on the grass and listening to a cuckoo than you can by studying Aristotle's *Ethics*. This amazing nonsense has seriously perturbed some of the poet's admirers; Morley tries to make out that he did not mean what he said, but Raleigh more wisely takes the bull by the horns, says he did mean what he said and was quite capable of talking nonsense.

That anyhow is Wordsworth's attitude, and I take it that it is very much the same as the Apostle's attitude in religious matters when he tells us to quench not the spirit.

Let your instincts have full play and don't apply your intellect to their conclusions. Dozens of people declare every Sunday that if you use your intellect you will go to the Devil.

"Spirit" and "intellect." There we come upon the great mental division which corresponds within our brains to the outward manifestations of poetry and science. It has become fashionable in some circles to talk about the difference between the "subliminal consciousness" and the "supraliminal consciousness," but these are long and clumsy words, and I prefer to call them for the purpose of this paper the "spirit" and the "intellect," assuming that I have Apostolic warrant at any rate for the former. This "subliminal consciousness" or "spirit" is that part of our mental activity which emerges in dreams and visions, partly under the control of the intellect often even then, and which creates the works of the poet, the artist, the musician, being then much more under the control of the intellect. "Let no man imagine," said Goethe, "that by the ordinary operations of the mind, or by any amount of thinking, he can make music like Mozart or pictures like Raphael." And indeed Raphael himself is said to have seen the Sistine Madonna appear visibly before him, he knew not how nor whence, and his active and conscious participation in the matter consisted merely in transferring his vision to canvas. So also in poetry the spirit supplies a constant stream of ideas and words and phrases, which the intellect controls, from which it selects and arranges, and which itself only partly understands. When these two work harmoniously together and the balance between them is perfect, then we get really fine poetry, but when one or the other predominates unduly, then there will be something wrong.

Blake is an example of the extreme predominance of the spirit. In Blake, perhaps more than in any other, we seem to get poetry in its purest essence now and then by fits and starts, but at an early age, perhaps from birth, something was wrong with his intellect. The longer he lived the more did he trust to the inspirations of his spirit, and the more he condemned the intellect, and Nemesis came upon him. From the enchanted *Songs of Innocence* he slid downward into the monstrous abortions of *The Marriage of Heaven and Hell*, and *Albion* and *Jerusalem*, and the spirit itself was wrecked for want of its pilot; instead of verse that ripples like a river, he pours out oceans of turbid stuff that is scarcely even prose. But as a rule what happens to poets is just the contrary. They begin with an excess of spirit in consequence of which they write harmonious magic without much content, then, if they are great poets, they arrive at the proper balance between the two faculties and write really great poetry, then in the third stage the intellect begins to get the upper hand too much, they may think more and may have more to say, but the natural gush is quenched and they write verse which is flat and feeble. This is particularly visible in Wordsworth himself; by an irony of fate he who had fought against the intellect was himself overcome by it; he who had kept on crying "Quench not the spirit" had his own spirit quenched by a thick blanket of moralisation and preachification, and the beauty of it was that he never knew what had befallen him. Browning is another conspicuous example of the same thing. These and many others go on writing verse all their lives, but in many cases the poet is wiser; feels the inspiration flag and betakes himself to something else; so for instance did Coleridge, Arnold.... But the great poets of the first order are those in whom the two faculties are in perfect harmony all their lives; there we get Sophocles, Dante, Shakespeare, Milton, Goethe.

This change takes place in all of us, or at any rate in nearly all of us. In youth we love dreams and delusions, we know nothing about logic or the value of evidence, we do not like to apply our minds to any hard thinking, and so far as we think about it at all we rather despise the operations of the pure intellect. The whole tendency of education is to correct this, to make us think, to make us work at intellectual things in an intellectual manner, to get us to look at things as they are, not as we should like them to be. It seeks to make us scientific instead of poetical, one might say; that is, it tries to correct the reliance upon instincts and make us follow evidence instead of impulse. Possibly it nips a good many youthful poets in the bud in consequence, but I do not think we need fear its doing any real harm in that way. For in the first place people with the poetic instinct but with no brains to speak of mostly let their education go to the dogs, and in the second place nobody is the worse for the loss of such; there are feeble minor poets enough about as it is in all conscience. And when you come to the great poets, the only ones worth troubling about, you find that they are eager to get all the education they can. Nobody can possibly be more educated than were Milton and Goethe.

In the poets of the first order, then, we find spirit and intellect walking hand in hand. They are not content with the one without the other. *They* do not think that there need be any conflict between the two, and so far from hating and fearing science, they embrace it eagerly. For that is the particular direction of all others which their intellect is apt to take. They want to know things, they are consumed by an insatiable curiosity. Before Dante and Goethe one stands aghast, in helpless amazement. They were walking encyclopaedias; whatever was to be known they had amassed and absorbed. Goethe is, of course, the grand example of the union of science and poetry. About the latter it is needless to speak, but I will briefly recapitulate his achievements in science, because to literary people they are but little known. Of their value indeed as advancing science it is difficult to speak, because there are very diverse opinions among scientific men on that point. But when all deductions have been made, it seems impossible to deny that Goethe more than any other one man founded the whole vast subject of the morphology of plants, a subject the importance of which was not truly understood before Darwin revolutionised biology, but which is now one of the staples of all botanical teaching and research. He is hailed, moreover, as one of the fore-runners of evolution, and though his ideas on that seem to have been of a hazy metaphysical kind in general, yet one cannot get over the fact that he definitely asked the luminous question which Darwin was to answer: "The question among naturalists," said he, "has been: for what does the bull use his horns? the question of the future will be: how did he get them?" It was Goethe who started the theory that the skull is a modified vertebra, a theory in which there has turned out to be a certain amount of truth.

Again, people used to assert that man was not made on the same plan as other animals, and pointed as a proof of this to the alleged fact that a certain bone was missing from man in the upper jaw; Goethe proved triumphantly that the bone was there. It is true that Vicq-d'Azyr had discovered it fifteen years before, but that does not alter the fact that the author of *Faust* made this discovery in human anatomy independently. All his life long he was absorbed in such things; for years he studied colours and wrote a great book upon them, but there he was frankly a failure, and as so often happens he was prouder of his failure than of anything else. "There have been greater poets before me and will be greater hereafter," he said, "but my glory is that I overthrew the Newtonian doctrine of colour." And again: "To make a name in the world you need two good things, a good head and a great inheritance; Napoleon had a good head and inherited the French Revolution; I inherited the Newtonian errors concerning light and colour." In his old age it became a mania, and his attitude upon the subject is distressing to his admirers. Geology, too, was a favourite subject, and when at the University he actually attended lectures on midwifery. It is this attitude of Goethe's which so vexed the soul of Mazzini. Commenting on his *Campaign in France* Mazzini cries indignantly, "Everything interests him, the skeleton of a sheep, the bones of a fish, everything except the movements of masses of men." And it is easy to see why Goethe could not tolerate the sort of windy atmosphere of gaseous gammon in which politicians dwell. I thought of that passage in Mazzini when I read a book by Wells called *Ann Veronica*. The heroine thereof after contact in London with politicians and suffragettes and such *bêtises* goes back to the room of Comparative Anatomy in this very College—and what a blessing she feels it to get back into that orderly domain, where something really is known, where one generation bequeaths its wisdom to another and one is rid of violent assertions about the unknown and the attitude of mad bulls in china-shops.

Therefore it was that that famous scene took place when a certain person went to Goethe at the time of the July revolution in 1830. A great dispute about cuttle fish had broken out at the same time in the scientific world in Paris and Goethe was full of excitement about it. When his visitor began talking about the importance of what was going on, Goethe said "Yes, indeed, it can no longer be kept hid—it will all to light" and so on, and the visitor couldn't make out what he was at, and began talking again about *his* exciting news. When Goethe saw what he was at, he said with great contempt "My good friend, I perceive that we are at cross purposes—I am talking not about these people at all, but about the report of St Hilaire; *that* is something important."

But Goethe may be exceptional, you will say. Take then Dante. The *Divine Comedy* is full of science, such as it was in the middle ages; in particular there is a most masterly résumé in the *Purgatory* of Aristotle's work in embryology, and in the *Paradiso* a most elaborate discussion of the markings on the moon. Dante wrote a scientific work himself; I do not mean the treatise *De Vulgari Eloquio* which is the first contribution to philology since the dark ages, the first extant since the *Cratylus* of Plato, but a less-known work, the question on Earth and Water. In the year 1320 Dante read at Verona an elaborate paper to prove that the earth sticks out of the water, not the water out of the earth. Such was the condition of science at that time that this was a disputed point, and Dante successfully solves the problem on the right side. Among other things he has to prove that water finds its own level. Imagine it! he must in all probability have been putting the finishing touches at that time to the ineffable last cantos of *Paradiso*, and yet he descends to discuss such a question as that with, to all appearance, just as much interest as when he is describing the mystic rose of Paradise in what is perhaps the highest reach of human song, in what is certainly unique in its ardent rapture and dazzling splendour in all the world.

And when we descend from the heights of Dante and Goethe, we find the same combination of interests in plenty of humble followers. Redi in the eighteenth century in Italy was a famous poet, but he not only wrote the delightful *Bacco in Toscana*, he also was the first man to knock on the head the theory of the spontaneous generation of animals which had been an article of faith ever since Aristotle, ever since the beginning of enquiry in fact, and which still flourishes in a certain corner of this College. Chamisso in Germany not only wrote the beautiful *Frauenliebe* which has been immortalised by Schumann's exquisite setting, but went on a scientific expedition to the South Seas and was one of the principal authorities on coral reefs before Darwin. Gray was a professor of history and drowned some of his poetry with it, but Gray was also an enthusiastic student of zoology and botany and according to his friends might equally well have been a professor of *them*. Tennyson is notoriously soaked in science; in fact a whole book has been written on his relation to it.

If we go back to the ancients we find the most remarkable instance of all in Lucretius, who wrote one of the great poems of the world on the atomic theory! It is true that the more scientific parts of that poem are the least poetical. Virgil in lines known to everyone regrets that the "cold blood about his heart" as he expresses it, prevents his following in the same line, but there is a certain want of sincerity in Virgil and I do not believe he was entirely serious in his complaint. Yet in several other passages he seems to think natural science is the ideal subject for a poet; such is the subject treated by Silenus in the *Eclogues*, and by long-haired Iopas in the *Aeneid*. Last, and dearest of all to me, Sophocles to one who can read between the lines is tarred with the same brush. Little things here and there show that he was master of the science of his times, such as it was.

This brief review is surely enough to show that the alleged antagonism between poetry and science simply does not exist. The names I have mentioned include four out of the seven great masters of European poetry, if we may take Tennyson's list as valid. Four out of seven is a pretty good percentage, and I think we may defy anybody to discover any other characteristic which marks so many as four of them—bating, of course, those special things in which every poet has got to be interested.

How different is the case if we look at metaphysics for example. Coleridge is, I believe, the solitary instance of any poet doing any kind of work in this line. Their general attitude towards it is rather that represented by Goethe, who told Jacobi that his metaphysical *tic* was a compensation for all the goods the gods had given him, "house, riches, children, sister and friends and a long etc., etc., etc. On the other hand, God has punished you with metaphysics like a thorn in your flesh; and me he has blessed with science, that I may be happy in the contemplation of his works."

What is the cause of this remarkable difference? The answer is obvious enough perhaps. The poet, the scientific man and the metaphysician are all alike consumed by the best gift nature can give to man, an insatiable curiosity; they all want to know things—at least most of them do. But the sort of things they want to know are distinct. The metaphysician wants to know some abstract truth, far removed from the panorama which nature spreads before him; the poet and the scientific man both want to know the panorama itself. They do not care about the abstract idea of ash-buds, nor the question whether the colour of the ash-bud exists only in the mind of the spectator thereof, or whether it has an objective as well as a subjective existence, or in general what is its relation to the percipient subject. No, but they like it as it seems to them, they note it as a living thing, and then use it as a simile:

More black than ashbuds in the front of March.

Everybody knows the old farmer in *Cranford* who had been walking among the hedge-rows for fifty years and never knew that, "and now comes a young gentleman from Cambridge and tells me that the ash-buds are black, and I look at them, and so they are." Professor Ker has observed that Pope is just like Tennyson in his noting of little things like that; only Pope as the poet of a frivolous society shows his observation on playing-cards instead of nature. That is the way of them all, more or less; they want to know the scientific facts, and they do not care about the rest in comparison. For the particular and the concrete is the life-blood of poetry, but the general and the abstract is death to it. Besides they want to know what can be known, and they think they see that metaphysic has only a doubtful claim to come under that head. Consequently their attitude to these mysterious subjects is apt to be one of agnosticism and indifferentism.

> When Bishop Berkeley said there was no matter,
> And proved it, 'twas no matter what he said.

And this type of mind is naturally led on to note the differences between the inflorescence of ash and of oak, to try and find out what are the natural causes at work in them, to devote itself in fact to science.

If then any poet attacks science, he is probably very young and his intellect has not yet begun to assert itself. So only can we excuse the extraordinary outbreak of Keats in *Lamia*:

> Do not all charms fly
> At the mere touch of cold Philosophy?
> There was an awful rainbow once in heaven:
> We know her woof, her texture; she is given
> In the dull catalogue of common things.

By "Philosophy," as the whole context shows, Keats meant science. Keats was surely the most glorious creature in himself whom we know of in our poetic roll since Shakespeare—if only he had had time to realise himself; but along with his radiant and supernatural splendours he had sad defects to which we may shut our eyes in reading him, but which we cannot ignore in applying to him the touch of cold philosophy. In particular we may say of him what Goethe said of Byron: "So soon as he reflects, he is a child." Why, at the very time when Keats was writing *Lamia*, a far greater poet than Keats was spending laborious days in investigating this very question of the colours of the rainbow—though to no good end. But Keats never lived to learn to think severely about anything; if he had, he might in poetry have rivalled Goethe himself. Of course the great comic poets jeer and fleer at science, as they do at other things; it is their business and it would be foolish to complain of them for it. What can be better fun than the *Clouds* of Aristophanes or the *Femmes Savantes* of Molière? Nay, Goethe himself can do the same when he likes; remember the scene between Mephistopheles and the student. But these people all do it in the right way, not like petulant children.

Akin to this notion that you cannot enjoy a rainbow properly if you know about the refraction of light is another heresy which is very common among the uninstructed. It is one which is always likely to be common because it appeals to two of the principal ingredients of the common mind, idleness and vanity. The heresy I mean is that you can enjoy things better if you know nothing about their technique; it is in fact simply the Wordsworthian doctrine about nature applied to art itself. It is, of course, in no way necessary to salvation to investigate the technique of verse; if any one likes to enjoy poetry and ask no questions, there is no reason why he should not behave in a concatenation accordingly. But he should not give himself airs about it, nor suppose that the application of the intellect to the works of the spirit will in any way interfere with his enjoyment. On the contrary, it greatly heightens the enjoyment; I do not say this depending on my own experience, but on the fact that the men who produce great poetry and who enjoy it most, one may suppose, are just exactly the men who do take interest in and investigate such things. And everybody who does understand the technique of any art whatever will bear witness that it adds to his pleasure. I will give two examples of the sort of thing I mean.

In Greek, Latin and Persian poetry a singularly beautiful effect is often gained by shifting the metrical accent and value of the same word when repeated; this can be done with ease in those languages because their poetry is quantitative. In English this effect can only be gained in a comparatively feeble manner and practically only with combinations of two monosyllables. A good instance is the first line of *Lycidas*

Yet *once* more O ye laurels and once *more*,

where the accent first falls on the *once* and the second time on the *more*. There are a great many instances of this in Shakespeare's sonnets. But perhaps the prettiest specimen of it I ever saw is in a poetess who was not by any means a great one, Mary Coleridge:

Over the blue sea goes the wind complaining,
And the blue sea turns emerald as he goes.

How beautifully there the change of the colour is echoed by the changing accent of the two words "blue sea."

My second instance shall be a method of expressing reflection in poetry, of which I know two very beautiful examples. Shelley in one of his most lovely lyrics describes the poet dreaming all day by the water side:

> He will watch from dawn to gloom
> The lake-reflected sun illume
> The yellow bees in the ivy-bloom.

No analysis can exhaust the charm of such lines; partly it is due to the repetition of the letter *l*, especially in the triple "rich rhyme" as the French call it, gloom, illume, bloom. That is why the bees in this passage are "yellow," not humming or buzzing or banded or fifty other words which would fill up the verse. But now for the way in which the reflection of the bees in the water is painted: "The lake-reflected sun illume." The enchantment of this greatly depends upon the fact that the second syllable of "reflected" itself reflects in a weaker form the sound of the word "lake," just as the water reflects in a weaker form the bees. If you doubt this, try the experiment of substituting any other word for either "lake" or "reflected" and see how the picture disappears.

My other example shall be taken from Shropshire. For Prof. Housman has now left us so long that we may be permitted to speak of him in this Society as what he is, the most exquisite poet of our own times. Two of the most beautiful lines in those beautiful if melancholy elegies are these:

> And like a skylit water stood
> The bluebells in the azured wood.

Here again is a reflection in water, and this time the magic effect is produced by repeating the syllable "like" inside the word "skylit," but inverted as a reflection is inverted in water.

Consideration of these details has led me further astray than I intended, and indeed there is no end to the mazes of this fascinating forest. Of course nobody ever yet wrote poetry by deliberately trying after such things: they are crystals created by the mysterious alchemy of the spirit, the intellect can only marvel at them. What the intellect has made, that the intellect can understand, but what the spirit makes is a mystery to it. Nobody will ever know exactly what makes the difference between a good verse and a bad. Spenser speaks of "the roses reigning in the pride of May," and everybody, I hope, can see what a line it is; it tastes like raspberry jam—why is "the roses blooming in the pride of June" such a bad one? Of course these delicacies are not *the* important thing in poetry; in fact there is a poetry which shoots up into an atmosphere where such ornament can hardly exist, a region crowned with snow, and much of the very greatest poetry is written in a style to which ornament is impossible. It would be so obviously to *King Lear*, to the passages in the *Prelude* about the soldier on the road and about the blind man in London, to the last lines of Emily Brontë, which I reckon to be probably the greatest short poem in the English language. All that I have been insisting on is that the analytic appreciation of the qualities and effects of the elements of verse is no hindrance to the enjoyment of the complete product, but quite the contrary. The more you *know* about anything the more you can enjoy it.

I have been dwelling on an application of science to poetry. Let us now consider the application of poetry to science. That poets are apt to be addicted to it I have shown, but how ought they to use it? Perhaps the less they use it, the better it will be for them and for us. In spite of Lucretius and Virgil science is not a fit subject for a poem, and those two giants alone have ever succeeded in doing anything with such a subject. The poet's business is to address the general public after all, and not to puzzle them more than he can help; he always does puzzle them of course, but that is because he *can't* help. But so far as he does touch upon science, it ought to be correct according to the lights of his time, and in the case of the great poets it always, or nearly always, is. If so, it becomes itself interesting to later generations. I have not often read anything more interesting than Psichari's papers on Sophocles and medical science, but they are so interesting because Sophocles was up to date in his medicine, and if he had not been so his science would have been simply a blot upon him and a nuisance to his readers. Again everything in that vast cathedral and store-house, Dante's *Divina Commedia*, is now interesting. Even the politics are so, even the Aristotelian philosophy or rather the blend of Aristotle and Christianity so cunningly compounded by Thomas Aquinas, even the exposition of the spots on the moon. All these things are now as dead as last year's cricket scores, and yet in Dante they are all alive. But it is because they do represent the truth as it was then not only to Dante, but to all the best men of his time. If they did not, they would simply bore us. It is amusing to compare the interest of these poets in science with the interest shown in it by their commentators. Virgil knew what was to be known in his time about bees, he loved them and was profoundly interested in them; but the modern commentator on the fourth *Georgic* does not seem to know the difference between a bee and a bull's foot, as the old saying goes.

It is true that there are certain poetic traditions which pass current because of their antiquity, mere commonplaces which nobody minds. Shakespeare may set a female nightingale singing with her breast against a thorn, if he likes. But when Wordsworth solemnly tells us that

> The blackbird amid leafy trees,
> The lark above the hill,
> Let loose their carols when they please,
> Are quiet when they will.
> With Nature never do *they* wage
> A foolish strife; they see
> A happy youth, and their old age
> Is beautiful and free—

then we cannot help being disgusted. It is not so much that Wordsworth knew nothing about "Nature red in tooth and claw" (though he might just as well have known that as Tennyson did), for the idea of the struggle for existence was not then familiar. But to talk about the beautiful and free old age of thrushes and blackbirds shows that Wordsworth was not up to the level of ordinary information and intelligence in his own times; Homer would have blushed to talk such nonsense. That I suppose is what comes of giving yourself up to poetical and natural impulse and neglecting science and the intellect. I am really sorry to knock up so often against Daddy Wordsworth, as FitzGerald called him; he was a most respectable old gentleman and he wrote some magnificent poetry, but it is hard to keep from laughing at him.

But a more common mistake is to drag in science *mal à propos*. When Tennyson says:

> The swallow and the swift are near akin,

one is shocked. It is pedantic and unpoetical. It so happens, too, that it is one of the few mistakes, I believe the only mistake, Tennyson ever made in science. So not even the ornithologist is pleased any more than the public is, for he knows that the swallow is no more akin to the swift than a hippopotamus is to a giraffe. But the moral on the whole perhaps is that if you are as great as Dante or Goethe you can do what you please; everything in such men is interesting, and you dare not meddle with it, and the longer time goes on the more interesting do they become. "You cannot touch it," said Heine of some passage, "you cannot touch it; it is the finger of Goethe." But if you are comparatively little, only a Wordsworth or a Tennyson, you had better mind your P's and Q's. And it will take you all your time to be only a Tennyson.

But there is no denying that the gradual growth of the intellectual powers and interests is a terrible danger to the spirit and to poetry especially. Few indeed are they who can hold the balance between them to the end, few highly favoured by impartial Jupiter. The classical example of such a downfall of, not poetic genius, but poetic taste, is Darwin himself; over and over again has it been commented on. When he was young he was an enthusiastic admirer of poetry, and one is not surprised to find in such a man, so remarkable for judgment and sense, that the poetry he admired was the best he knew. He was not taken in, as scientific men so often are, by the third and fourth and tenth rate—indeed nearly all young people are so taken in, even if they flatter themselves that they are poetical and thank God that they are not as these scientific students—no, but his particular idols were Milton and Shakespeare. When he was absent from England on the famous voyage of the *Beagle*, if he went on an expedition and could only take one book with him, that book was Milton. In his old age he laments pathetically, with that charming humility which made him the most lovable of men, that he had entirely lost this taste. He had been peculiarly fond of Shakespeare's historical plays, but on looking at them after an interval of many years, found them so dull that, says he, "they nauseated me." Remembering the condition of his health, I think the phrase is to be interpreted quite literally. And it is really no wonder. For many years, under constant pressure of wretched health, he had been struggling to work at scientific questions, and everybody knows what an astounding work he had done. It is not strange at all that he should have lost a taste which most people never have to any extent worth mentioning, and which most of those who do have it lose in later life without any excuse at all. And indeed one is often tempted to think that such a mind as his exceeded in the grandeur, sublimity and simplicity of its ideas the imaginations of any poet. But he grumbled himself that he had become a mere machine for grinding out general laws. Anyhow it is quite certain that if you want to retain the taste you must cherish it, or it will die away. And cherish it how you will, you will find it change.

Gibbon observes of Claudian that he does not often satisfy or silence our reason. No poetry can ever satisfy the reason, but it can silence it by, in a sort of way, hypnotising us. Certainly good poetry throws one into a sort of trance, and if the trance be deep enough the poet may defy reason in the most audacious manner. Perhaps the most astonishing instance of this is the adventures of Odysseus as recounted by himself in the *Odyssey* ix–xii; for obvious reasons I will not dwell upon these books, but will take a parallel case from Shakespeare. When Othello is asked by what magic he secured the love of Desdemona, he answers by telling us that he talked to her about his own adventures. That is natural; the reason or intellect has nothing to say against it. But watch how he continues:

> The Anthropophagi, and men whose heads
> Do grow beneath their shoulders. These things to hear
> Would Desdemona seriously incline.

Well, if Othello had really told Desdemona about such things, she would have laughed at him, let us hope, instead of seriously inclining. Yet it is all right, and nobody ever cavilled at it. And the reason why is that the intellect is entirely caged and bound by that magnificent scene, and in the second place the instinct of both Homer and Shakespeare has acted in the same way: they both make the hero tell these stories, but do not themselves represent him as doing these things; the impossible is removed into a distance and can be accepted. In fact Shakespeare could not even have made Othello tell Desdemona such stories upon the stage, or he would be hissed off it. It would be like Mr Hoopdriver telling Jessie Milton how he ate stuffed ostriches at the Cape. When on the other hand the battle of Shrewsbury is actually represented on the stage, with kings and princes whacking at one another like common soldiers, the intellect is disgusted; the play degenerates into a wretched farce. I don't know how I could live without Sir John Falstaff, but when I come to that battle I skip over it as fast as I can and cannot pretend to like it. It does very well for boys. But there is no saying where to draw the line. When I was a boy myself I could read the whole of *Paradise Lost* with equanimity, even the battles of the angels with their gunpowder. Now I confine myself to about half the poem.

As one gets older and the intellect more and more asserts its sway, these misfortunes are bound to happen; common-sense rises in revolt against the spell of dreams. If it is allowed to have its head, it may end by shattering the talisman, and that is what one must guard against. But *if* one sticks to both one gains more, much more, than one loses. One learns the difference between the best and the second best, a difference which young people hardly ever know. *You* all know it, of course, but it is not all young people who are endowed with your instinct. Outside this Society I think you will find they *don't* know the difference, as a rule. Certainly I did not—it wasn't only *Paradise Lost*—I did not see really the difference between Shakespeare and Marlowe, nor between Shelley and Swinburne, nor fifty other like cases. And I have observed that always without exception I have ended by coming round to the general opinion of the world; you can easily be cleverer than one man, said La Rochefoucauld, but you cannot easily be cleverer than the world. And the best becomes a treasure such as one never dreamt of.

In the second prologue to *Faust*, the prologue on the stage, in which is packed together perhaps more wisdom and shrewdness, more common-sense and knowledge of the world, and more poetical beauty than can be found in an equal space anywhere else—in that prologue the poet, regretting the loss of youth, says of himself as he remembers himself in that delightful period:

I had nothing, and yet I had enough,
The impulse towards truth, and the delight in illusion.

There in a nutshell is all I have tried to get clear, at, I fear, undue length. Goethe retained both all his life; try to do likewise.

CAMBRIDGE PRELECTION

(5th Nov. 1921)

Cambridge Prelection on Plato, Phaedo, *chaps.* 45–48,
pp. 95 E–100 B

I HAVE chosen to speak upon these chapters on this
occasion mainly because I think that I have a good deal
to say of them which is new and important; partly also
that it is a melancholy satisfaction to me to discuss in this
University a passage in which I first became interested
under the guidance of that great man[1] who has left a void
which can never be filled, and upon whom so many of us
will look back with affection and veneration to our dying
day. I never propounded my own theory upon it to him,
for by the time I had elaborated it he was too ill to listen,
and it is entirely different from his own views.

95 E. The point at which we have arrived in the dialogue
is this. Socrates has put forward the first proof of the
immortality of the soul, namely the proof which is given
by the combination of the two theories of antapodosis and
anamnesis. He has then added supplementary evidence of
a general kind to show that soul is altogether more divine
and more permanent than body. The majority of his
audience were apparently convinced, but the two Thebans,
Simmias and Kebes, still raised objections. Simmias produced the old theory that the soul is merely a name for the
harmonious tempering of the bodily elements, as a lyre may
be said to have a soul when its strings are tuned in any
given musical mode. This has been quickly disposed of by
Socrates to the satisfaction of Plato, perhaps hardly to the

[1] Henry Jackson, Regius Professor of Greek 1906–1921.

satisfaction of his readers. But the objection raised by Kebes seems even to Socrates to be really fatal to the proofs which have been offered since the conclusion of the argument from antapodosis and anamnesis.

I observe parenthetically that Kebes has certainly not overthrown that argument; he has not even attacked nor so much as mentioned it. The reason for this omission— surely a very strange one if you look on the conversation as a real one—is purely dramatic; it is as if you were first to prove Euclid i 47 as Euclid does, and then add some vague arguments which are *not* mathematical proofs, and then some one were to attack the latter without a word of the former, and *then* all the audience should be downcast, not one of them remembering Euclid's proof. I do not go further into this point here, but call attention to it as one of the many proofs that Plato writes as an artist, not as a historian, throughout this dialogue, and that it is quite impossible to accept it as a true representation of anything said upon the last day of the life of Socrates. So potent is Plato's magic that he carries every one away and they do not notice it. Kebes however certainly shows that the supplementary evidence put in by Socrates is defective; it only proves that soul is tougher and longer-lived than body, it does not prove that death may not after many conflicts advance his pale flag over the soul herself. In order to prove that soul is really immortal and imperishable, Socrates will have to show that death cannot under any circumstances whatever enter into the soul, that nothing can bring about her destruction, that no *cause* can be found sufficient for this, seeing that the *cause* of life is necessarily and eternally exempt from all contact with the cause of death. "What you desire to know, Kebes, is no trifling matter," says Socrates (95 E); "it involves nothing less than raising the whole question of the causation of generation and destruction."

With a view to leading up to his own account of this causation Socrates then gives an account of his own experiences. So says the Platonic Socrates. But it has been long an article of faith, alike with ancient and modern expounders of Plato, that what the Platonic Socrates says need not be taken to apply to the historic Socrates; that in the earlier dialogues indeed he may be only a glorified presentation of the real man, but that in *Meno* and all the later dialogues he is mainly a mouthpiece for proclaiming Plato's own theories.

Lately an attempt has been made to maintain that this is a mistake, that what Socrates says is to be taken quite literally as representing the views of the real Socrates, dressed up no doubt in flowing robes and ornamental attire and put into a literary form, but still substantially historical. To defend this position it is necessary to throw overboard the evidence of Xenophon as worthless, as merely the vague reminiscences and deliberate fictions of a rather stupid military man with no turn for metaphysics; it is necessary to belittle the express statements of Aristotle, who had every opportunity for being well informed on this point, and who was neither stupid nor military nor unmetaphysical; it is necessary to fly in the face of Plato's own equally express statements in the *Apology*, surely a more historical work on the face of it than the *Phaedo*; it is necessary to ignore the fact that in all Plato's earlier works there is not a word to be found about the theory of ideas either earlier or later, and that we can see him gradually excogitating it in (for example) the *Euthyphro*. This attempt therefore, in spite of the high authority of its daring authors, may I think safely be dismissed, and in the course of what I say I think I shall provide further proof of its impossibility.

If however the passage is not a history of the thought of the real Socrates, the obvious alternative is to suppose that the experiences of Socrates as here narrated are really those of Plato himself. The difficulties in the way of believing this ἁπλῶς will be developed in the course of my comments on the account here given. For the moment I will only say that I believe the greater part of them to be nothing of the kind, but part really to be so.

Plato wants to prove the immortality of the soul, and he thinks he can do so by developing a correct theory of causation and applying that to this particular question. Now what is the natural thing to do if you are going to put forward a new theory of causation? What for instance did Aristotle do in like case? The answer is evident; he wrote the first book of the *Metaphysics*, reviewing therein the theories of his predecessors from Thales to Plato. I quote his own words from the beginning of that book:

We have studied these causes sufficiently in the *Physics*, yet let us call to our aid those who have attacked the investigation of being and philosophised about reality before us. For obviously they too speak of certain principles and causes; to go over their views then will be of profit to the present inquiry, for we shall either find another kind of cause or be more convinced of the correctness of those which we now maintain.

He points out that the early Ionians or hylozoists only looked at *one* cause, the material; that Anaxagoras introduced two new causes of the very greatest importance, the efficient and the final, but that Anaxagoras failed to work out the latter or to apply it to his theories of cosmogony and of the ordinance of the Universe; that Plato then added the last, the formal cause.

Now is it not as plain as daylight that all this is exactly and precisely what the Platonic Socrates does here in *Phaedo*? I say it is as plain as daylight—but for years I used to knock my nose up against all this, like a pike in an aquarium. Like Aristotle, Plato wants to preface his own theory by a review of his predecessors and of their theories. But Plato at this period of his life was a great dramatic artist, the greatest and most fascinating of all dramatic artists who ever wrote in prose. Therefore he does not give us a dry matter-of-fact statement of what Thales said or what Anaximander said, but, seeking as ever to make his exposition lively and not reckoning on the dulness and lack of imagination which unfortunately are only too prevalent among mankind, he turns the whole story into a sort of allegory; the slow course of thought as developed by one school of philosophers after another is condensed into a fictitious account of the wanderings of one soul in quest of truth, and that soul is of course called here Socrates, for the purpose of his dialogue. Certainly I do not mean that Plato supposed the individual generally to go through this development; he never did go through anything of the kind himself in spite of his being at first a disciple of Cratylus; I mean that it is more lively, more interesting, more poetical if you like so to call it, to put the work of generations into the pretended reminiscences of an old man calling it all up as his own past.

No doubt he could have made Socrates recount it all as dryly as Aristotle does. But could anybody have thanked him for it if he had? None who has ever read it can forget how the Athenian youth heard some one reading from a book of Anaxagoras (as he said), how his heart was filled with the prospect of a glorious truth to illumine and redeem all the world, and how the cup was dashed from his lips. As soon should we forget how he pressed down the springing curls upon the neck of Phaedo. By this fictitious setting Plato has burnt what he had to say into our brains; such is the power of imagination. But it needs imagination to answer it; he who comes to knock at Plato's door without that will not perhaps go empty away, but he will not divine the true meaning of the oracle. When I say that imagination is needed, I only mean that you must put yourself into Plato's position, see what he was aiming at, see why he chose to put things as he did. There is another representation of Socrates in literature which makes the same requirement, and which shows the amazing liberties the Athenians took in such matters—the *Clouds* of Aristophanes, which I here allude to because you there have a pretty close parallel to this passage of the *Phaedo*. Whereas Plato represents a number of different theories which belong to a number of different persons as *succeeding* one another in the development of the mind of Socrates, Aristophanes represents him as holding a number of theories of other persons all at the same time. Why did the poet attribute all that amazing farrago of nonsense to Socrates? Not because Socrates really troubled his head about such things; he neither investigated, as Aristotle might have done, the *incessus pulicum*, nor taught rhetoric like Gorgias.

Everybody knew this. But Aristophanes wanted to attack the whole tendency of the new thought; to do this in accordance with the methods of the Old Comedy, it was not merely convenient but absolutely necessary to embody those tendencies in one man. Granted that, all the rest follows; Socrates was the only man he could by any possibility have picked for the part. What Aristophanes did on the stage, Plato in his own way has done for the closet or the lecture-room; both of them make many voices speak from behind the mask of Socrates.

So much for preliminaries. I propose now to give you a brief summary of my interpretation of all this passage. It will be necessary to make so many digressions and speak on so many topics that, to use a homely phrase, you might not be able to see the wood for the trees if I did not first sketch out the main outline; you will then be able to follow me filling it up. Thus do I translate the essential portions of the story into the historical truth which it has so long disguised like the sun in an eclipse. Indeed I conceive that I am doing what the great Aristotle did, for I believe that in the first book of the *Metaphysics* he had all this passage in his mind and was playing his usual game of reducing to black and white what Plato left glowing with iridescent fire.

96 A. The question raised is the question of the causation of γένεσις and φθορά. I (Plato) will give a sketch of the views of my predecessors on this. When Philosophy (not Socrates) was young it was wonderfully enamoured of this which they call natural science, thinking it a fine thing to know the causes of phenomena.

96 B. Accordingly different thinkers put forward dif-

ferent views. Some for example said, as Anaximander, that animals were formed out of decaying matter; Empedocles said that we think with the blood, Anaximenes with air, Heraclitus with fire, Alcmaeon and the medical school with the brain.

96 C. But in the end this early school of natural science was convicted of incapacity by the criticism of the Eleatic philosophers. Owing to its persistently looking at only material phenomena and material causes, it was so stupefied that it could not even explain why a man grows. Anaxagoras had said, and it had certainly seemed reasonable enough, that it was because particles of flesh, bone and so on in the food we eat were added to the flesh and bone in our bodies. But when the Eleatics propounded their arithmetical puzzles, it became evident that the natural science philosophers had no answer to give them; they could offer no explanation for instance of how one and one become two. So feeble was their notion of causation.

97 C. A far nobler and more brilliant theory of causation was however put forward by Anaxagoras; it was only thrown out in an isolated manner and had no connexion with the rest of his speculations or with the Ionian school in general, but noble and brilliant it was. Reason, said he, ordered all things with a view to the best.

98 B. But unfortunately he did not apply this theory to his explanation of the universe in detail; he only talked of material causes like any other Ionian.

99 D. Plato himself would have liked to follow up the hint of Anaxagoras, but did not see how to do so. He fell back therefore upon the next best theory which he could devise. Physical science having failed in the investigation

of the truth of things, he took warning by the fate of his predecessors, and feared that he like them might be blinded in consequence of tackling physical phenomena with his senses. He sought refuge therefore in λόγοι, assuming the truth of the Theory of Ideas as the strongest he could attain to, and putting down as true whatever agreed with it. And in particular he asserts that the true theory of causation is that which makes the phenomena depend upon the Ideas.

Now let us go back to the text.

96 A. "When I was young," says Socrates, "you cannot believe how enthusiastically I pursued this wisdom which they call the investigation of nature; I thought it a glorious thing to know the causes of everything—why each thing comes into being, why it is destroyed, and why it is. Many a time and oft did I swing to and fro from one theory to another. Are animals formed by putrefaction of the hot and the cold? Do we think with the blood, or is it by means of air, or fire? Or are all these views wrong; does the brain produce in us the sensations of hearing, sight and smell, and thence arise memory and opinion, and knowledge springs again from these when they have settled down? Such were the questions I asked, and I asked too what again destroys all these things; and I searched out the phenomena of the heaven above and the earth beneath. And what was the end of it all? Why, I found myself the stupidest creature in existence in these investigations."

There, I say, you have Plato's history of the Ionian philosophy, including the medical school of that period. And you have his terribly severe indictment of it—it turned out to be the stupidest creature in existence. He does not put it in chronological order like Aristotle, but he quite agrees with Aristotle in substance. The early philosophers set out to discover causes of things, *rerum cognoscere caussas.* When Virgil wrote that famous line was he not translating this very phrase of Plato's, ὑπερήφανον γάρ μοι ἐδόκει εἶναι, εἰδέναι τὰς αἰτίας ἑκάστου? And the only sort of cause they could suggest was a material one. As for the reason why the question what we think with is made so prominent, it is surely obvious that Plato lays particular stress on this *one* question because he considers the inadequacy of the material cause to be especially glaring here, as indeed it is; "I cannot conceive," said Huxley, "how matter can think."

"It is as if," says Socrates presently, "you should say that I sit here because of my bones and sinews, not because of my sense of duty." So to say that the cause of *thinking* is blood, as Empedocles thought, or air as Anaximenes, or brain as Alcmaeon of Crotona, is an even more inadequate statement than to say that earth and water are the cause of our bones. Therefore it is that Plato picks out this special point for emphasis.

With regard to the alternatives proposed, it is interesting by the way to see that Plato allows the medical authorities a place. It appears to have been Alcmaeon of Crotona, that shadowy elusive alluring figure, who if we could only get a better sight of him might perhaps be rightly called the Harvey of the ancients—*he*, I say, first clung obstinately to the view that the brain is what thinks, but the philosophers have never been willing to admit it. Plato however had the sense (at any rate in his later days) to take his physiology from Hippocrates, and was not inclined to ignore the medical faculty as completely as many of his brethren. The conflict between the two parties is very visible in Aristotle and elsewhere; how eloquent is the fact that he never mentions Hippocrates but once, and that in the *Politics*! The medical writers retorted by ignoring Aristotle's science, so there is not much to choose between them. But all that is another story, which this is no place to go into.

Here Plato dismisses both classes of speculators with equal contempt. Neither Ionian science nor Italian medicine find any favour in his sight. Socrates found himself the stupidest creature in existence. In modern language and properly interpreted this statement is only another way of proclaiming what has been called the "bankruptcy of the Ionian science."

And what convinces him of stupidity? Listen to his own words (96 c):

My sight was so blinded by this enquiry that I unlearnt again even what I thought I knew before. For example, why does a man grow? I had supposed it obvious to anybody that it was because of eating and drinking, that particles of flesh and bone out of our food were added to our own flesh and bone, and so on with the rest of our bodies, that this process of addition resulted in making a small mass into a large one, and that this was how a small human being becomes a big one.

But, he continues (I will not go minutely into what follows), he gave up this plain and simple view because he got involved in logical puzzles, such as that addition of one to one cannot make two, in which for all I know Mr B. Russell and Mr Whitehead may agree with him.

I must enter into several digressions here. There is a point of great importance. The theory about the flesh out of the food being added to the flesh in our bodies is that of Anaxagoras, and so far as we know of nobody else. Socrates therefore is already acquainted with the philosophy of Anaxagoras. Yet we shall be told presently that he knew nothing of his book and apparently had never heard of his name. This is very strange if we suppose all this history to be that of the mind of the real Socrates or of Plato himself. It is worse than very strange, it is a flagrant self-contradiction. Hence Mr Archer Hind denies that we have here a reference to Anaxagoras at all, and thinks that this is simply the common-sense view of the average unthinking man. But that can hardly be the case. The average man does *not* think that flesh and bone are in bread; so far from that it does not appear that Anaxagoras ever converted anybody to this opinion. But this self-contradiction is quite natural if we suppose, as I do, that Plato is giving in a parable the history of philosophic thought. This part of the speculations of Anaxagoras is quite germane to the rest of these purely material causes, and Plato was perfectly justified in committing this little anachronism, he who did not care a snap of the fingers for anachronisms, whatever Wilamowitz may say.

There is another interesting point to make here by way of parenthesis. Lucretius asserts that the meaning of the homoeomeria of Anaxagoras is this:

> ossa videlicet e pauxillis atque minutis
> ossibus hic et de pauxillis atque minutis
> visceribus viscus gigni (putat).

If now we compare the words of Lucretius with the words of Plato we see the Latin to be virtually a literal translation from the Greek. That means, I take it, that both Plato and Lucretius, which is to say Epicurus, are quoting the very words of Anaxagoras with their curious plurals σάρκες and *viscera, ossa* and ὀστᾶ; curious because they mean *bits of* flesh and *bits of* bone as well as flesh and bone as wholes. In any case I can have no sort of doubt that the reference here *is* to Anaxagoras.

And there is another point of some consequence. M. Tannery, a name never to be mentioned without respect, and certain eminent authorities following in his wake, have declared that Aristotle misunderstood or at any rate misrepresented the doctrine of Anaxagoras by describing as material particles what in reality were only qualities. Anaxagoras talked of "the hot" and "the cold"; Aristotle substituted material atoms and thereby took in and deceived the whole world. I am astonished again at the easy way in which we moderns throw over the authority of Aristotle whenever it suits our convenience, and I cannot believe that the ancients who followed Aristotle were so ignorant as not to know that they could buy the works of Anaxagoras for a drachma at the outside and confute Aristotle from the original text. Well, but here Plato says exactly the same thing; *he* also talks of material particles, not of qualities; will it be asserted that it was Plato who "went about to banter the world with an enchanted" Anaxagoras transformed from the real thing?

The real truth about it seems to me obvious enough. Try to put yourself into the state of mind of a man thinking about these questions at a time when there was no word yet invented for *matter*, no word for *quality*. Speech creates thought, as Shelley says; when a vocabulary is not yet developed, thought suffers and is cast into dire confusion. These early speculators had no word for *matter*; consequently they call it "the hot and the cold" and such phrases; how then could they help confusing matter and quality? This confusion crops up in many places; it is at the bottom of the four elements of Empedocles, which have no sense in them except as signifying the four conditions in which we know matter, and yet you know that is not what Empedocles meant by them; it is at the bottom of the Aristotelian doctrine of the four elements, a doctrine which is not much to its author's credit, with its jumble of earth and water, air and fire, hot and cold, liquid and solid. No wonder then that Anaxagoras also, who had not the advantage of the Aristotelian vocabulary, groped about in the dark and did not distinguish properly between σπέρματα of gold, and its qualities. But to the minds of Plato and Aristotle the distinction was clear, as it was to Democritus; if they choose to speak only of the material particles of Anaxagoras and to say nothing about their qualities, that is their own affair, but they were in their rights; a modern investigator ought to distinguish sharply between the two, dividing them with a hatchet, to adopt the old philosopher's own metaphor; but he ought *not* to cleave to the one and ignore the other, nor to accuse Aristotle of reckless misinterpretation.

Early philosophy then had thought that a body grows greater by addition of particles to particles. Then it found itself stranded in a mist of metaphysical puzzles. (The coming of metaphysics upon the scene is like the coming of the Albatross to the Ancient Mariner.) Precisely then came the Eleatic criticism of the earlier thought, in particular Zeno, the founder of dialectic as Aristotle calls him, Zeno who revelled in arithmetical quibbles. Of him has it been written that men were doubtless puzzle-headed before him, but nobody ever had such a capacity for bringing out that quality, and that is just what he does here. My interpretation of all this passage then is simply this. Ionian philosophy thought it knew certain obvious things, such as the cause of growth as expounded by Anaxagoras. Then came the criticism of the Eleatic school and showed that people could render no intelligible account of even the addition of two units to make two.

Philosophy in their hands began to turn from contemplation of the material universe to contemplation of logical questions. The eternal dispute whether Zeno should be placed in order of date before Anaxagoras is of course an uncertain question, but it is not a matter of any consequence for our present purpose. Anyhow Plato handles these matters freely. If he represents philosophy convicted of stupidity by the Eleatic criticism before he introduces the new cause of Anaxagoras, this is not necessarily because Anaxagoras preceded Zeno, if he did precede him; it is because he wants to finish off his criticism of the first stage in the history of causation before he goes on to the second. It is quite immaterial to his purpose to ask whether Zeno really perplext men with his problems before Anaxagoras wrote.

Next therefore we now come to the famous passage in which Socrates heard one reading from a book the epoch-making words: "Mind came into Chaos and ordered all things for the best" (97 B *ad fin.*). καὶ οὐκ ἂν ἀπεδόμην πολλοῦ τὰς ἐλπίδας..., "not for a great sum," says he (98 B), "would I have parted with the hope I then conceived. In great excitement did I lay hand upon his books as soon as I could get them, and began my reading that I might know

at once the best and what is worse than it. High indeed
were my hopes, my friend, and great was my fall, when
as I advanced in my reading I found my author making
no use of his mind whatever" (there is here a play on the
words "his mind" which has generally been missed), "nor
bringing into play any causes fit to be called *causes*, but
airs and ethers and waters and other such absurdities."
Plato then proceeds to his severe criticism of the failure of
Anaxagoras to apply his idea, his new cause. But he does
not deny the importance of this cause; in his opinion it
is *the* cause which is the highest of all, and if a man could
but gain a knowledge of it he might count all else as dross.
ἐγὼ μὲν οὖν τῆς τοιαύτης αἰτίας ὅπῃ ποτὲ ἔχει μαθητὴς
ὁτουοῦν ἥδιστ' ἂν γενοίμην· ἐπειδὴ δὲ ταύτης ἐστερήθην
καὶ οὔτ' αὐτὸς εὑρεῖν οὔτε παρ' ἄλλου μαθεῖν οἷός τε
ἐγενόμην, τὸν δεύτερον πλοῦν ἐπὶ τὴν τῆς αἰτίας ζήτησιν ᾗ
πεπραγμάτευμαι βούλει σοι, ἔφη, ἐπίδειξιν ποιήσωμαι;

"Most gladly," says Socrates, "would I sit at the
feet of any one whatever who would teach me the truth
about it. But since this was denied me, being unable
either to discover the truth for myself or to learn it from
any one else, I have contrived a crutch instead to aid my
steps in the search. Shall I explain its nature to you?"
(99 c).

Before going further, I wish to call attention to the fact
that we have here applied to a particular case a general
principle laid down some way back. At 85 c Simmias has
observed that certainty in this life upon such questions is
difficult, perhaps impossible; "yet" says Simmias, "it
would show a sad want of grit in a man not to thrash out
the current statements about them, declining to give up

the attack before he is exhausted by investigating the question on every side. For it is our bounden duty to bring to pass one of these three things, either to *learn* the truth or to *find* it, or (if we can do neither of these) at least to take hold of the best and most inexpugnable of theories (λόγος) known to man, to ride upon this as upon a raft and sail through life trusting in it at all hazards." Why this general principle should be given to Simmias to proclaim is rather puzzling at first sight. Anyhow here at 99 D we find all the conditions fulfilled; Socrates can neither *learn* nor *find* the truth; he is exhausted by investigation; therefore he falls back upon a λόγος. As Simmias had described this λόγος as a raft, a makeshift when no better vessel is to be had, so Socrates describes his own procedure as a δεύτερος πλοῦς, rowing when he cannot sail. This comparison adds further proof, if further proof were needed, that the δεύτερος πλοῦς means "a second best course."

But in truth the principle was not altogether new to readers of Plato, for part it had been laid down in the earlier dialogue of *Meno*; Simmias therefore is perhaps only repeating what he had learnt before as a member of the Socratic circle, just as he repeats elsewhere what he had picked up from the Pythagoreans. There is no originality about him anywhere. It is first laid down in *Meno* by Socrates himself; being presumed familiar it is now put into the mouth of a secondary character—so delicate are the links which bind the Platonic dialogues to one another.

We come now to the well-known passage which has been the despair of commentators, 92 D. If my view of the proper interpretation of the whole story of the adventures is correct, it should enable us to throw some light upon these crucial sentences, and I am bold enough to think it does. I will go through them piecemeal and minutely.

First of all, we must ask what is the exact meaning of τὰ ὄντα. There has been considerable difference of opinion on this point. It means τὸ δέον καὶ τὸ ἀγαθόν, says Mr Archer-Hind; Socrates wanted to see that the view of Anaxagoras was the right one, and that all was regulated for the best. Others say it means simply "things." I hold that the latter view is the correct one, for these reasons. If τὰ ὄντα meant the true essence of things, τὸ δέον and τὸ ἀγαθόν, Plato would have made this clearer; he would have said at least τὰ ὄντως ὄντα. And he uses τὰ ὄντα about a dozen times in this dialogue, and in all those passages it means simply "things" in the widest and vaguest possible way—it may include the ideas in one place and implicitly exclude them at another, but it is just like the English "things" and never means the reality behind them as distinct from them.

But if τὰ ὄντα here means nature in general, *not* the glorious revelation promised by Anaxagoras, it follows further that we are not continuing the thread of the previous paragraph at all. For the connexion of thought we must regard chapters 46 and 47 as parenthetical; the beginning of ch. 48 articulates in reality with the end of ch. 45. The whole passage about Anaxagoras is an episode and excrescence on the main history. And so the theory of Anaxagoras was.

And by the way I cannot resist the pleasure of quoting from Sir Herbert Warren's reminiscences of Mr Bywater the sentence: "I well remember especially how he brought out with great *empressement* the appearance of Anaxagoras and his discovery of νοῦς which made him appear like 'a sober man after the wild talk of his predecessors'" (*Life*, p. 69). The book of Anaxagoras belonged in its details to the same category as the books of Anaximenes, Empedocles, Democritus; it was of the earth, earthy. The single hint which it threw out about some higher cause was no doubt a brilliant flash, but it never came to anything and did not disturb the current of Ionian philosophy from its bed. Plato has done it full justice, as he always did in speaking of his predecessors.

Observe indeed how wonderfully Plato has treated it from the purely artistic point of view. The other early philosophers are identified with the poetical and mythical story of the adventures of Socrates, but the episodic nature of this outburst on the part of Anaxagoras is brought out strongly by the device of making Socrates hear somebody else reading it out of a book. It comes in from outside like a bolt from the blue, it is weighed in the balance and found wanting as applied by its author, and now we drop it again altogether and go back to the main stream of the history.

Socrates then continues thus (99 D):

It seemed to me at this stage, since I had failed utterly in the investigation of things, that I must be careful lest I should share the fate of those who contemplate and examine the sun in eclipse; for you know they sometimes ruin their eyes unless they look at the sun's image in water or some similar mirror. So I too bethought me of something of this kind; I feared lest I should utterly blind my mind by looking at things with my eyes and seeking to grasp them with each of my bodily senses.

There is a serious confusion in the expression of this

paragraph. "I thought," says Socrates, "*after* this, that I ought to be careful. I feared lest I *should* be blinded by examining nature in the Ionian manner. I feared this *after* I had failed in looking at things." Let me offer a respectful parody of this. "I spent ten years in playing cricket without pads, and found it painful. After this, when I had given up playing cricket in consequence, I feared lest I should hurt my shins, and so I took to another method and adopted the use of gloves."

The editors skate hastily over this thin ice, and hold their peace. Let us see whether any explanation can be given of it; the contradiction is there and cannot be explained away. I have tried hard to get round it and I cannot see how it can be done. In such a case there are three roads open: first, we can shut our eyes and pretend that nothing is wrong; secondly, we can proceed to do violence to the plain meaning of the words and twist them into something we prefer; thirdly, we can acknowledge that something *is* wrong and then try to explain *why* the author put it wrongly and how the trouble came about. For myself I greatly prefer this third course, and I think that we really can see very easily *how* it was that Plato came to express himself in this manner, illogical as it seems at first sight. Interpret Socrates again into terms of the first book of Aristotle's *Metaphysics*.

When the Ionian philosophy had broken down in its effort to explain the universe, being reduced to absurdity by Eleatic criticism, Plato next thought the right plan was to seek refuge in the theory of ideas. For Plato thought that the material method could only blind the soul by turning its gaze earthwards; accordingly he fled for shelter to the ideas.

You see now, do you not, how the contradiction arose? Socrates stands neither for the son of Sophroniscus nor yet for Plato himself, but for the history of philosophy down to and including Plato. Now it is quite natural to say that the Ionians failed in their investigations and that Plato learnt wisdom from their failure and consequently took care to avoid falling into either the error of the gross dealers in material objects, or the error of Anaxagoras who thought he was going to storm heaven right away with his theory of Mind ordering all to a good end. But when both the Ionians and the Eleatics and Plato himself are all identified for dramatic purposes with one solitary individual, then the allegory, as allegories will, breaks down. It is possible that Plato might have avoided this awkwardness if he had liked. But I imagine that he did not care to trouble himself about it. For one thing he rather had a fancy for puzzling people, and if that was his object he has certainly succeeded.

Socrates stands for the Ionians. Therefore it is necessary that he should fail after protracted endeavours to get at truth with his material causation. Socrates stands for the Eleatics. Therefore he has to convict his Ionian self of stupidity by mathematical puzzles. Socrates stands for Plato himself. Therefore he has to take warning by his Ionian self, and avoid studying the very things at all from the beginning which, as typifying the Ionian philosophy, he had been studying for years and years with all his might.

That is what comes of writing allegories. But the game is worth the candle; who would not rather read Plato's allegory than Aristotle's sober statement of fact? Plato knew well enough that the contradiction was there, I do not see how he can have helped knowing it; but he did not think it mattered; how he would have been amazed to see the way in which he has been interpreted by the literal moderns! That is what comes of expecting other people to possess imagination.

But after we have cleared up all this confusion we are bound to enquire what is the meaning of the parable of the astronomers and the sun. "I feared lest I should share the fate of those who contemplate the sun in eclipse, for you know they sometimes ruin their eyes unless they look at the sun's image in water or some similar mirror." I think it has been shown pretty clearly that the meaning of Plato in this passage is simply that after the Ionian philosophy had failed, because it only recognised material causes, he (Plato) therefore took up an introspective line of enquiry. It has been shown, if I have been successful so far in my endeavours, that there is here no question of the sublimer cause of Anaxagoras. Therefore it follows that the simile of the sun is not to be pressed, that we must not seek for some explanation of it which will represent Plato as fearing that he would be blasted by the excess of light of the Anaxagorean νοῦς. It has been truly observed that astronomers only look at the sun in eclipse or at least did in those days, and that accordingly Plato need not mean anything subtle by adding the word ἐκλείποντα. This view is borne out very strongly by a passage in the fifteenth chapter of the Life of Pythagoras by Iamblichus, which is plainly written with the Platonic passage in mind.

"Pythagoras was of opinion," says Iamblichus, "that other men must be content to gaze upon the Creator in

P   14

images and patterns, δι' εἰκόνων καὶ ὑποδειγμάτων, for their benefit and instruction, because they are not able to attain to the pure and original archetypes, just as those who are unable to gaze stedfastly upon the sun by reason of the surprising splendour of his beams have eclipses shown to them in a deep pool of water or by means of melted pitch or a dark mirror."

I gather from this that the forgers of Pythagorean Apocrypha plundered this passage of *Phaedo* among so many others and ascribed its doctrine to their own hero, and *they* did not understand the reference to the sun in eclipse to have any profound significance.

At the same time I cannot agree with those who maintain that the expression δεύτερος πλοῦς and the simile of the sun are both ironical. I see no sign or symptom of irony in the whole passage. Plato really would have liked to see the ἀγαθόν of Anaxagoras if he could, but he does not yet see his way to doing so; in the *Republic* he does see his way, as he thinks, thanks to the invention of the Idea of Good. Meantime the δεύτερος πλοῦς really is a second best course, and remember how he asserts in the *Republic* that the most noble and lofty of his ideas only derive their value from that Idea of Good. So also Plato wanted to know the truth about things; he believed this truth to be something inexpressibly magnificent; both the garment of the outward universe and the mirror of our own minds are reflexions of this; in both alike a man may well seek for revelation. But experience shows him, as he thinks, that looking at material things will *not* lead to such revelation; on the contrary it only blinds the mental eye of the enquirer. That is just what metaphysicians go on saying about natural science to this day. Our only course is to give up physical science therefore and take to mental; not that mental is in the least inferior, as he is careful to add. ἴσως μὲν οὖν ᾧ εἰκάζω, τρόπον τινὰ οὐκ ἔοικεν· οὐ γὰρ πάνυ ξυγχωρῶ τὸν ἐν τοῖς λόγοις σκοπούμενον τὰ ὄντα ἐν εἰκόσι μᾶλλον σκοπεῖν ἢ τὸν ἐν τοῖς ἔργοις: "perhaps the simile is not perfect; for I am very far from admitting that he who considers things in propositions is viewing them in images more than he who views them in actualities" (99 E).

We may here well ask a question; what is the connexion of these clauses? "My simile is not exact. For λόγοι are no more εἰκόνες than τὰ ἔργα." If this refers only to the words beginning at ἔδοξε χρῆναι, then there is no connexion, no coherency at all. Therefore this refers to something more: what Plato says, or should have said, is something like this: "λόγοι are εἰκόνες of the truth, and I fled for refuge to them because I feared being blinded by the phenomena, which however are also only εἰκόνες of the truth, although I did just now compare them to the sun itself. That was an oversight which I now correct." If you will consider carefully that clause οὐ γὰρ πάνυ ξυγχωρῶ you will see that it is absolutely necessary, if you want it to be coherent, to assume that the sun represents τὰ ἔργα for the nonce. And Archer-Hind was therefore wrong in contemptuously throwing over that notion. But Plato has, perhaps on purpose, been a bit careless in expression, as people are in developing their ideas in real speech. Socrates *ought* to have said that the truth which lies behind and gives rise to both material and mental phenomena is like the sun. He is still struggling in the confusion into which the allegory has thrown him, and I do not see how it can be denied that he has got into another confusion between being blinded by poring on things and being blinded by gazing at something too bright. At any rate I cannot see my way to getting this passage clear and can only console myself by reflecting that no one else can either.

But it will be said that Plato does not take such an indulgent view of the phenomenal universe as I have here represented him to have taken. No, not in certain of his later writings; but in *Phaedo* he has not yet proceeded so far as he does later. In no early work of his does he express an opinion that the world of matter is so contemptible as he declares it to be in the *Republic*; neither in *Phaedo* nor in any other earlier work does he say that the material universe is intermediate between Being and Not-being. The one truth which underlies both nature and mind is one and the same; both are manifestations of it; if you can get at it through either, do so by all means, but as a matter of fact you can't get at it by physical science: *that*, as I conceive it, is his attitude at this period. Then he becomes more and more contemptuous of material phenomena, but the *Timaeus* is enough to show that to a certain extent he reverted in his age to the position of his youth. He always looked with dislike upon matter; but he could not and did not deny that it was an outward and visible manifestation of the reality he sought; the earth spirit weaves for God the garment thou seest him by; the material object exists because it participates in or copies the idea. But if you want to know that idea you must look rather within than without.

I suppose I ought to give here my reasons for assuming the *Republic* to be a later work. I am fully persuaded that it is such for these reasons: (1) The psychology of *Phaedo* is less developed than the psychology of the *Republic*. (2) The tenth book of the *Republic* is of the nature of an appendix to *Phaedo*, as well as to the *Republic* itself; now it is evident that at the same time it is an integral part of the larger work and that Plato never intended to stop at the end of the ninth book; therefore, if he added a supplementary proof of immortality in that tenth book, it shows that *Phaedo* was already published, and indeed he actually as good as quotes *Phaedo* in 609 D and as good as refers to it by name in 611 B. (3) In *Phaedo* he has not been able yet to link together the cause of Anaxagoras with his own theory of Ideas; in the *Republic* he has succeeded in doing so by the Idea of Good. (4) In *Phaedo* Socrates is still a real man, and the dramatic setting of the dialogue is masterly; in the *Republic* Socrates is a mere vehicle for Plato's own notions, and the author has largely lost his interest in the dramatic side of the dialogue; he has become more of a preacher and less of an artist. (5) This very comparison of the truth of things to the sun is here confused and sketchy, I might say unintelligible; in the *Republic* VI it is elaborated and vastly improved. (6) In *Phaedo* the ideas are still of an ethical and mental kind only, ideas of equality and the like; in the *Republic* we hear of ideas of all kinds of things, cats and dogs, even manufactured articles.

Had the *Republic* been the earlier dialogue of the two, it would have been difficult to avoid supposing that the sun of the one illumined with its light the sun of the other. But if the truth is the other way about, we need not suppose any connexion between the two. For in the earlier work we have here merely a casual illustration, which has not *yet* become a matter of any importance.

100 A.   ἀλλ᾽ οὖν δὴ ταύτῃ γε ὥρμησα...

"However that may be, such was the line I took. Not only in regard to this question of causation but in regard to every other I assume as my starting-point the theory which I judge to be the strongest. I then put down as true or false whatever appears to me to be or not to be in harmony with this. But I should like to explain to you more clearly what I mean; for I think you do not see it at present."

"No indeed," said Kebes, "I do not."

"Why, this is all; no new thing, but what I have continually told you before and have never ceased repeating in the discussion to-day. So I will now proceed to try and disclose to you the sort of theory of causation which I have struck out for myself; I will return to that old story of the ideas and begin with them, assuming the existence of absolute beauty and goodness and greatness and so on; if you allow their existence, I flatter myself that I can explain thereby my theory of causation and discover a proof of the immortality of the soul."

I also will go back to what I have been saying before; look again at 85 c *fin.* "One must lay hold of the best and most inexpugnable human theory one can get, and rely upon that." "If indeed," Simmias says there, "we had a revelation from heaven, that would be another matter." Plato, then, represents Socrates here as still carrying out the scheme laid down by Simmias. He has failed himself, has had no divine revelation from either Anaxagoras or anybody else, and so he falls back on the best human theory he can get, which for Plato is of course the theory of ideas.

It may again be objected that Plato would never have spoken of this, the theory of ideas, as a δεύτερος πλοῦς or as inferior to anything whatever. But I entirely disagree with this view. Plato really did see the difficulties in the way. What is the meaning of the whole vast and perplexing dialogue *Parmenides*? As I interpret it *part* of the meaning is just this: "There are desperate difficulties in the way of the theory of ideas; I (Plato) see them as well as anybody. But there are equally great difficulties in the way of other theories too, which nevertheless are true. For example, look at the One and the Many. It must needs be true that either the One or the Many exist. Yet take which alternative you please, it can be made to appear impossible. Therefore the fact that human reason cannot understand a theory plainly or make it intelligible does not prove that it is untrue. So I cling to my theory, and do not care what you say."

Such I conceive to be part of the meaning of the *Parmenides*, though one may well speak with trembling of that formidable work. Anyhow Plato was already alive to the troubles of his theory when he wrote *Phaedo*. For in 100 D he virtually confesses that he cannot make up his mind on the question how the ideas make the particulars, "whether it be by indwelling presence in them or communion with them or what and how you please to call it." It is just this problem which he lays such stress upon in the early part of *Parmenides*. He cannot yet make up his mind what is the truth about it when he writes *Phaedo*; whether he saw as yet the difficulties so plainly and had stated them to himself so forcibly as he saw and stated them in *Parmenides* cannot be decided with any degree of confidence. But that he did already see them is, I think, indisputable. Nevertheless he does stoutly maintain that in default of anything better he must sail through life (as he expresses it) upon this raft; he must assume Truth, Goodness, Beauty and such essences to be the reality of things, to lie behind them and give them whatever excellence is theirs. And then he will proceed to argue about other questions on this assumption, "putting down as true whatever agrees with it."

The method looks a terribly unscientific one, and Plato might have learnt better from his master. Certainly Socrates was not in the habit of arguing thus. I imagine him heckling Plato on the point and insisting that the first thing to be done with a hypothesis is to cross-examine it and, if it will not hold water, to give it up. And the fact that the Platonic Socrates here professes without a blush that *he*, he of all men! invented this other method, is a knockdown blow indeed to the notion that we here have a truthful account of the development of the real Socrates.

And yet it is the way in which people do argue, even in the highest scientific circles. When gallium was discovered it fitted into the periodic law, and the chemists were highly pleased. When argon was discovered it contradicted the periodic law, as it seemed, and what did the chemists say? "Give up the hypothesis? Not we. There is something wrong somewhere, but it is not in our hypothesis." And Wisdom was justified of her children on that occasion. Like Plato, they assumed their hypothesis, believed what agreed with it in the case of gallium, and refused to believe what did not in the case of argon, nor did they rest till they had coaxed argon into agreeing too.

This method is not therefore by any means so crude and desperate as it appears at first sight. But it is *not Socratic*.

However, that is how we are to prove the immortality of the soul. Granted the theory of ideas, Plato proceeds to apply it to the question on the lines laid down by Simmias in the passage I have already quoted more than once; what agrees with his hypothesis he puts down as true and so by one of the most terribly inconclusive pieces of argument ever seen establishes what he set out to prove.

The Pythagoreans, it is to be observed, have never been alluded to, even in the most distant manner, in the whole of this history of the theory of causation. This is certainly somewhat strange. Aristotle gives them a prominent place —nay, he declares roundly that in Plato's theory "only the name 'participation' was new; for the Pythagoreans say things exist by 'imitation' of numbers, and Plato says they exist by 'participation,' changing the name" (*Met.* I 987 B 10). Of course the answer to this is that Aristotle speaks of the Platonic theory in its later development; he is aiming particularly, as is his wont, at the contemporary Platonic school, in particular Xenocrates, with whom the numerical and Pythagorean aspect of Platonism had become so important. In the theory as we see it in *Phaedo* there is nothing due to Pythagoreanism. And if it be said that anyhow Plato ought to have mentioned it in writing a history of causation, I answer that he was not bound to mention every school; he is treating the subject very freely and giving a sketch of the general tendency of philosophy; he was no more bound to mention Pythagoras than to mention Leucippus. So far as the general tendency went the Pythagoreans were open to the criticism here passed on everybody before Anaxagoras; they, the Pythagoreans, only knew of a material cause, only their material was number and their numbers were material. But they never spoke of a final cause at all, and it is the absence of a final cause that is the great blot on all these early systems in Plato's opinion.

If it were really true, as recently maintained with great learning, that Socrates got the theory of ideas from the Pythagoreans, then it *would* indeed be strange that they should be here omitted, and the fact that they *are* omitted is one of the most deadly arguments against that theory.

It is quite true that Plato here represents himself as being driven to the Ideal Theory by perplexities of a mathematical kind. At least he says that the material cause, or rather the material and scientific (as we should now call it) way of looking at things could not explain for him how one and one become two, and so on. But these puzzles are not Pythagorean, they are Eleatic. If we may take the statement at the end of chapter 45 to be auto-biographical, as perhaps we may, then *it was the Eleatic impulse and no other* which drove him to the Ideas. And therefore he might well speak as he does elsewhere of "his father Parmenides." Nor would this contradict in any way the account given by Aristotle, for what Aristotle says at the beginning of the sixth chapter is that Plato's system "in most respects followed these thinkers, but had peculi-arities which distinguished it from the philosophy of the Italians." By Italians he means Eleatics as well as Pythagoreans. He then adds what the other influences were, to wit, the Heraclitean doctrines taught to Plato by Cratylus and the search of Socrates after the universal in ethical questions. But the real connexion of Plato and Pythagoreanism is rather that the later Pythagoreans stole from Plato, as we have just seen in the simile of the eclipse, not that Plato stole from Pythagoras, except in one point, which I will admit to be as important as you like— namely that he mixt up Pythagorean arithmetical non- sense with his ideas in the later and esoteric development of which we know nothing except what Aristotle tells us.

And the conclusions we may draw from this interpre- tation of the whole passage are:

First, that it is not of any avail to appeal to this sketch of the history of philosophy in order to draw any inferences from it about the teaching or the thought or the develop- ment of the real Socrates. Indeed the real Socrates, the son of Sophroniscus, does not appear in the allegory at all: we jump in it straight from Anaxagoras to Plato him- self. And this was necessary; Plato could not bring in Socrates for the simple reason that Socrates took no interest in such questions. What he thought about them appears very plainly from the statement of Xenophon, which there is really no reason to doubt; *Mem.* I i 14. The substance of that statement is that Socrates thought scientific specu- lators no better than madmen, for some of them thought one thing and some another exactly contrary to it, for example one set asserted that everything γίνεσθαι καὶ ἀπόλλυσθαι and others that nothing could ever do either the one or the other. These were the opinions of the historical Socrates about γένεσις καὶ φθορά, that nobody knew any- thing about them. And if he had read the *Phaedo*, he would, I fear, have thought Plato just as mad as the rest of the philosophers.

Secondly, that Plato did not regard himself as affiliated to the Pythagoreans, but as being led to his theory of causation by the Eleatic criticism of the physicists, and by the Eleatic logical puzzles. And this agrees excellently with the way in which the Eleatics are brought into connexion with the Ideal Theory in *Parmenides*. It was only in later days that he began to draw in an evil hour upon the magic fountain of moonshine which had sprung up in the Pythagorean school.

Such is my view of the true meaning of this enchanting but enigmatic passage, such are the conclusions which I hope may be legitimately drawn therefrom. It is just possible that some of my audience may have grown a trifle rusty in their Greek philosophy and may have found it difficult to follow me in all the ramifications of my exposition: if so, I apologise to them and trust they will forgive me for endeavouring to make a serious contribution on such an occasion to a great subject, even at the expense of their convenience.

For EU product safety concerns, contact us at Calle de José Abascal, 56–1°, 28003 Madrid, Spain or eugpsr@cambridge.org.

www.ingramcontent.com/pod-product-compliance
Ingram Content Group UK Ltd.
Pitfield, Milton Keynes, MK11 3LW, UK
UKHW012331130625
459647UK00009B/202